*Letters
to Saints
and other
Sinners*

Also by H. S. Vigeveno

Climbing Up The Mountain
Jesus The Revolutionary
Thirteen Men Who Changed The World
Sinners Anonymous
The Listener
Is It Real?

Letters to Saints and other Sinners

H. S. Vigeveno

A. J. HOLMAN COMPANY
Philadelphia · New York

U.S. Library of Congress Cataloging in Publication Data

Vigeveno, H. S.
  Letters to saints and other sinners.

  1. Consolation 2. Pastoral counseling. I. Title
BV4905.2V54   248.4'8'51   70–39415
ISBN-0-87981-006-8

Contents

Introduction

What do you say to a father who discovers that his son is on dope? To a man who maintians his innocence while serving time in jail? To a mother whose son is killed in the war? To a girl who can't say "no" to men? Or to a person who has lost his faith?

I have attempted to face these and a number of other problems, simply and honestly, from may personal counseling and small group experiences. I hope that these letters will give both insight and help to those who may be facing similar crises.

All names have been changed to protect the guilty.

My thanks to all those who encouraged me while these letters were being broadcast in Southern California; to my wife who has been a constant source of encouragement and help; and to Miss Janis Dunham for her good work in aiding the preparation of the manuscript.

Letters about Family Problems

"*The house of the wicked shall be overthrown: but the tabernacle of the upright shall flourish.*"

Prov. 14:11

1

Letter to a
Busy Father

Dear Joe,

Your letter landed like a bombshell on my desk, and I can imagine the agony you felt as you wrote. You convey your shock and surprise, and I can see why.

Isn't it strange how we can breeze through life, kept busy by the responsibility of making a living, when suddenly in a crisis like this we raise the basic questions: "What's it all about? What is the purpose of life, after all?"

So you've discovered that your son is on dope, and you didn't even suspect it. Now all your talking with him isn't doing a bit of good because you've drifted apart. You can't reach him since he won't let you. Did he really say it was too late? At sixteen? Even if he did, you must not accept such a statement as final.

The main issue is, of course, that he doesn't want help now. But let me point out at once that deep down he really does. He may not admit this even to himself, but ask yourself, Joe, why

11

is he on drugs? His experimentation is a reaching out, a desire for new experiences he thinks he is missing.

How could he ever get involved? Well, you know, drugs are readily available on campus. There is a staggering increase in the influx of drugs here in Southern California. One year the police seized 120,000 units of narcotics and two years later it was 7,500,000! And they say that's only about ten percent of the traffic. No wonder many parents are concerned. The question is why didn't we become concerned when we first heard about this growing problem?

You have something else to contend with—the curiosity of youth, the natural rise of temptation. Of course we've always fought those battles even when you and I were teenagers. But all that propaganda about dope and all that talk about marijuana and speed offer a growing enticement to our youth. When an announcer on T.V. steps up to the mike saying, "Hi, and I am, and I'm glad I am," doesn't it make you wonder what we're coming to?

Now I suppose you could scare him a little, but I doubt if it will have much effect. I read of a bright, college freshman who was an heir to his parents' fortune. (His father had built an university in New Jersey.) And this Freddie III (I'm deliberately changing his name) died from an overdose of opium derivative and L.S.D. in a dormitory room on the campus. Eighteen going on nineteen.

But the larger question, Joe, is why? Why do we have to have our kicks? What was missing in Jerry's life that he had to experiment with dope? What weakness in his character led him to get hooked? What was denied him that he had to seek this form of escape?

Those are the questions which are bugging you, aren't they? I know, because you've tried to be a good father. You've always wanted your children to have religious training, but you did let them drop out of church some years ago. They had their excuses about the church being too strict for them, and so on, but isn't that another symptom of our sick society? We're so overly permissive that the kids run the country instead of the other way around. They want to dictate to our schools, and it all begins when we allow them to sit at the top of our family totem pole. They know when they're up there and have their say, so it shouldn't surprise us that such things are happening in an overindulgent and careless society.

But this is hardly a nice way to talk to you since you're in big trouble, although the authorities haven't picked him up yet. Incidentally, there are some youth who secretly wish that something would happen to them. Why? They yearn for some authority figure to set his foot down, to keep them in line. Like the young child who was bugging mamma all day and finally settled on the sofa with: "I wish Daddy would come home and *make* me behave."

One of your pressing questions is, why is he doing this and why won't he quit. Perhaps he *can't*. He may be hooked. And, as you know, it's no easy matter to kick the habit. There are some agencies that can help him, places where he can weather the withdrawal periods, and where he can talk over his problems, but he must be willing. That's first. And when he gets to that point you can talk.

His argument that "grass is not as bad as war" is beside the point. Of course it's not as bad because it isn't killing other people, but it is a slower form of murder. He is actually killing himself, deliberately. And if he won't get off the stuff, he may never live a normal life. His argument may be that he doesn't want a normal life (like you), but I'm talking about a meaningful life.

He will not only kill himself, but all those around him. . . with the hurt and pain he inflicts. He's never thought about it that way, not really thought about the many lives he touches. He says that he loves because he's really turned on now. If he really *loved* people, would he so selfishly want to hurt them?

Psychologists point out another interesting behavior pattern. When we are afraid of something, we want to prove to ourselves that we can handle it. And we have to prove it over and over again. Maybe you didn't measure up, you didn't make the football team. Even after you were rejected, you kept on throwing a ball to prove to yourself that you could pass well or catch. I heard one observant black man say that he had never met a militant person who was not a coward at heart. You see? Trying to prove he's not a coward.

Take the sex athlete. They're trying to prove to themselves over and over that they're really men (or desirable women), because they secretly wonder if they are!

Jerry may be trying to prove something to himself. He may be scared. He probably thinks he doesn't measure up in our society, and here is one way to achieve recognition. Now he belongs with a group, a way-out, groovy group. He didn't make it in sports. He didn't make it with the good guys. He didn't make it scholastically. So for the moment he's found his niche, and he is actually too scared to face life without that protection.

You can see that he needs a lot of help, and that means there *is* something you can do for him. You can build up his confidence. You can help him to realize that he doesn't have to run scared. You can identify with him. This is going to be hard for you, because he won't let you get close to him. But don't hide your feelings, Joe. In group therapy with adolescent drug users, these kids often express their need for closer relationships. You'll have to take more time with him, but that will mean examining your own goals, won't it?

In some parts of the world parents are held accountable for their children. When a young person commits a serious wrong in the East, the parent is disgraced before the community. I'm sure that you hold yourself somewhat accountable. You've been very busy. You've made it in your business, and it hasn't been easy. You've driven yourself unmercifully to get to the

14

place you are. You've been home very little, often coming in late, leaving early and hardly joining in for any meals with the family. Even on weekends you had piles of work around you.

You didn't have time to romp on the floor with your children when they were young; you didn't have time to play ball when your son was eager to. You were on the move and Martha let you drive on. She understood and accepted you, but your children didn't understand. Nobody could change your obsession to succeed. And whenever you did let down, you just folded into your armchair, turned on the T.V. and wanted everyone to be quiet. So they went off to their rooms and the family drifted apart.

How much time do you spend with them now, Joe? You find time for golf and some games with the alumni at the stadium, but even on the weekends you are thinking about Monday. When do you really have time for Jerry? He needs you now. It isn't too late yet, but you'll have to take a long, hard look at your commitments.

We live in such a fast-paced society that it becomes necessary to gain a new perspective. But I remember reading somewhere that the things our children recall are not necessarily our living room furniture, the color of their rooms or the new shower we installed when funds became available. What they do recall are the times spent together as a family. Was the home a home, or was it merely a boardinghouse? Was there a family unit, or just a group of people sharing the same living quarters and going their separate ways?

Jesus once said that a man's life does not consist of the abundance of the things he possesses. We need to ponder that in our culture. What are our values anyway? What is of utmost importance? What really counts in the long run? What does it mean to lay up treasure in heaven rather than on earth, where moth and rust corrupt and thieves break through and steal? What is the implication of not being overanxious about tomorrow? How can we seek instead the kingdom of God? Are we so

15

busy adding things for ourselves that the kingdom of God is placed way out there as an extra? Jesus reverses the field. He turns our values upside down!

I keep thinking, Joe, that if we will take Him seriously, our lives can move in the right direction. If we will seek the kingdom of God first, these other things will fall into place. I'm not suggesting that all Christians will be devoid of trouble, or that a Christian parent will never have a son on dope. Not so. There's more to this business of being Christian parents than simply calling ourselves Christians.

I am saying that if we conscientiously and seriously attempt to follow Jesus, to put His teachings into practice, to make Him Lord of our lives and therefore do what He counsels us to do, that our values must change, our lives must change and also our relationships.

A president of a small Christian college was asked why his four sons all grew up without getting into trouble. They never seemed to rebel. He replied that he didn't know, but that he had asked one of his sons about it once. His son had not pointed to their church attendance or the pattern of regular devotions around the dinner table. He said: "You and mother are so happy at home together."

Don't give up, Joe. Jerry is still young. No matter how strong his desires are now, there is a greater drive within him. It's the desire to live a meaningful life. Why is this stronger? Because God put it there, and there is always hope that this God-given incentive, created within us, will win the day.

Some people call this "your better self." I call it an awareness of God. It is that God-shaped void which only God Himself can satisfy. But all this need for God is presently overlaid by Jerry's problem. It *is* a foreign element. It *is* an overlay. Like sin in the human blood stream.

Now Christ has come to take away our sin. He died to remove the disease of sin itself. Our constant struggle is for victory, not defeat; for life, not death. "Man was not made for

16

defeat," wrote Hemingway. If you will join in that struggle of faith, I'm certain there will be help and hope for your son. For God "is able to do immeasurably more than all we can ask or conceive, by the power which is at work among us" (Eph. 3:20, NEB).

Yes, Joe, I'll join you in prayer for him as you request, and I hope that you will also put your prayers to work!

Sincerely,

2

Letter to a Disturbed Mother

Dear Jean,

When you wrote a few days ago I began to see how you have held in your emotions and have always found it difficult to express your conflicts. Jean, everyone considers you such an easygoing person, managing your home and your affairs so well that it will come as a surprise that you have obviously bottled up your frustrations. But you are beginning to realize that it can never turn out well to keep all that inside. A pressure cooker builds up all that pressure, but if the lid would ever blow off, there would be an explosion in the kitchen.

Your letter was one means of allowing some of that pressure to escape. I liked that ray of sunshine when you admitted that you knew you weren't the only one with problems. Of course. Wasn't it Thoreau who said that we all fight battles of quiet desperation? There is so much going on beneath the often calm, smiling masks people wear.

Rare are those people who have no financial worries! Even

the wealthy are unsatisfied, particularly those who have made money their aim. Most couples seem to have too little money left at the end of their budget. Or they don't have a budget. Of course there are many unforeseen expenses with children, and you and Paul have been trying to make ends meet. But just as you think you get them to meet, someone is always moving the ends! That's the price you pay living in our ecomony. It isn't for nothing that T. S. Eliot calls the major sin of the twentieth century—avarice.

But you are more worried about the guilt you feel because you are not working. You are not contributing financially to the family budget. Yet, suppose you went out to work? Many a mother feels guilty about leaving the home and family, because she can't be there for her children. There's no need to feel inferior when somebody asks you what you do and you reply: "Oh, I'm only a housewife." *Only?*

When your children come home from school, you're there, and they are a little more secure knowing you are. I saw a paper that an eight-year-old wrote about mother: "A mother is a person who takes care of her kids and gets their meals, and if she's not there when you get home from school, you wouldn't know how to get your dinner and you wouldn't feel like eating it anyhow." I think the most important part of that sentence is that *you wouldn't feel like eating it anyhow!*

But your children give you problems too. You wonder if the situation will ever improve. Well, Jean, no matter what age they are, there'll always be some problems. You encountered them when they were still babies, you experience them during elementary school and you are just beginning to discover some of the teenage tensions. But parents tell me that they are concerned about their children even when they get away from home, and grandparents worry by proxy.

As to Paul, you want to know whether you should avoid little grievances, overlook petty annoyances and not discuss them with him. You're afraid they will cause hard feelings between you, and so you've simply kept them to yourself. But you don't want to become like the wife who never argues with her husband and lets him yell it off. Then she goes ahead doggedly with what she wants to do anyway. Besides, all this is churning within you and you're getting sick of it.

Now, I don't think that either money, the children or your husband are your big problems. It's these inner frustrations. How much easier it seems for us to point to others as the reason for our distress. How much more difficult to search within. You say that you are held under the circumstances, but why do you allow your circumstances to dictate to you? Why are you *under* the circumstances? You are inwardly annoyed. That's the real issue. And isn't this what you are trying to tell me, actually, in your letter?

As you face all this honestly for the first time, you recognize that you are in reality not this calm, collected person your friends consider you to be. You have been avoiding your problems. You have not dared to look into a mirror. It's been too unpleasant. And as long as you keep walking past a mirror, you never see yourself. Why? Because you are probably afraid. You sense (as we all do) that the image is not very flattering. But when we look at ourselves as we really are, we take the first step toward healing.

Can you begin to discuss this with Paul? He is your husband, and you surely communicate with each other about the children, the home, and family matters. Can you approach a more honest relationship in which you are helping one another to understand each other? Isn't this what marriage should accomplish? Are we not united for the purpose of understanding, sharing, growing, maturing, healing and forgiving? Isn't this part of the oneness we read about in the Bible, when God states that two shall be one?

You can never be satisfied with a marriage that merely exists on the surface:

"How have you been?"

"Fine."

"Had a good day?"
"Yes. And you?"
"Well, the kids were a problem. Jimmy..."
"Oh, that's too bad."
"Well, I told him he could see no T.V. tonight."
"O.K. That'll make it a bit more quiet after dinner."
"Oh, Paul. I wish you'd look at the bathroom faucet."
"Yea."
"It's dripping again."
"Hmm, hmm."
"And the screen door still isn't closing properly."
"O.K."
"And..."

So, turn the television off, sit down and talk, but don't you do all the talking! Have you ever asked yourself why you neglect this necessary communication? Perhaps one of the reasons is that you're really afraid, afraid of him, afraid he won't approve, afraid he'll be hurt, afraid he won't understand, afraid he'll criticize you. And he may feel afraid also!

Let's overcome this fear. How? By stepping out on the thin ice of communication. Once we dare, we may discover that the ice is more solid than we imagined, and it will hold us up.

But, Jean, you have written to a minister and obviously you think that I will be able to help you through the Christian faith. You feel so guilty. You want to be able to face yourself. But how can you live with yourself with this new insight? How can you keep the pressure from building up all the time? How can you be free to cope with everyday situations? These are your real questions.

As long as you think that the problem is somewhere out there (which you don't), you will never find any answers. You are the key—and God alone can offer you forgiveness so that you will be able to live with yourself. How often I've seen the miracles take place, the miracle of grace that sets a person free. But how?

21

You cannot do it alone. It may help to see a psychiatrist and understand why you build up this pressure. Still, that won't be enough. What do you do *after* you understand? Forgiveness, removal of guilt and freedom come from another source, from outside yourself, from God.

This is why you asked me how God can forgive you. You are very hard on yourself, Jean. Perhaps you expect too much. Perhaps you have set impossible goals which you can never reach. Perhaps you need to be more realistic. But consider how you accept your own children. You don't want them to carry a burden of guilt. You don't want them to bottle up their feelings. You want them to learn to live in freedom and love, and to accept your forgiveness. You may temporarily punish them or correct them, but your motive is love and your real feelings are those of concern and care.

God is our heavenly *Father*. (That's what it means to be a parent.) And He does not want us to exist with guilt and fear and frustration. Take a good look at Jesus. He expresses the love of the Father. Aren't you struck by one overwhelming fact, that Jesus did not make people feel more guilty than they already were? He never made anyone feel guilty, except those religious hypocrites who approved of themselves already. Everyone else Jesus accepted readily, in spite of their sins, whether a woman taken in adultery, a greedy little swindler, or a notorious criminal condemned to death. Their main problem was to accept the love which He freely offered. And they did!

The Father who Jesus reveals by His life and death, is the Father who cares for His children and loves His world. He loves it so much that He sent His only Son to die for us all. He wants us to experience freedom from guilt. He did not come to trap us, but to free us. And if that story of the prodigal son who runs away from his father's house is true, if that father really accepted his son with open arms when he returned, then we must actually accept in faith what Jesus tells us. *Jesus* tells us this. He who comes from God! On His authority we may believe, for we all want to return home!

We can come home. Jesus has made it possible. He has opened the door to the Father's house. He is the door and the way. He has died on the cross for us. He has taken our sins. He has accepted the responsibility: Christ was innocent of sin, and yet for our sake God made him one with the sinfulness of men, so that in him we might be made one with the goodness of God (II Cor. 5:21, NEB).

That's not only the goal. That can be a present reality. If only you can see it that way.

And now comes the next step. Having accepted God's forgiveness, you must also accept yourself! If He accepts you, even though He knows all about you, who are you not to accept yourself? To forgive yourself? Only one thing can keep you from taking that step of forgiveness—pride. Your own ego prevents you from slipping into this true freedom.

Freedom can be yours. Jesus has said that He came to set us free (see John 8:32). Only we ourselves block the road.

Many people have trouble at this point, and as I said, pride is the trouble. I'd simply ask you to ponder this truth: If God accepts you, who are you not to accept yourself? If God Himself forgives you, who do you think you are not to forgive yourself? So, have you really accepted the love of God expressed at the cross? If you have, the other should follow!

This will not be the complete answer to all your problems, Jean. But it's the beginning, the new birth, the opening up to a new life in freedom. Not allowing the pressure to build up, but letting the steam escape because you are free.

It is like a birth, both the agony and the ecstasy of it. You remember about birth, don't you? You remember how it was with your babies? And the great fact is that birth brings new life into being. New life—new and free.

May the Lord be with you.

3

Letter to a Couple on the Brink of Divorce

Dear Betty and Bill,

It was good to be able to talk with you when you came to see me the other day, but I wanted to follow up with a letter since I didn't have a chance to answer some of your questions. In sharing your conflicts with me, you made a concrete attempt to avoid a divorce. And in spite of the seriousness of your situation, that was an important step. Would you agree that most couples entertain the possibility of divorce at some time during their marriage?

Of course it's not difficult to obtain a divorce. Lawyers know the technical language, and it doesn't take much to turn your back on a troublesome relationship. One lawyer has a sign on his door which reads: "Satisfaction guaranteed or your honey back." The real trick in life is to find satisfaction without going to court and losing your honey. But that's why you came to talk, wasn't it? Your objective was to discover some way through your conflicts.

As happens quite frequently with couples, you repeated the

phrase: "But we don't seem to love each other any more." Yes, if falling in love is as heady as the songs and movies tell it, it is a cinch to fall *out of* love too. But love is more than something you fall into and out of. Love isn't just receiving a good feeling. It's giving. Love isn't what you get from marriage. Love is something you give to marriage, and you keep on giving continually, willingly, without grudging.

I'm sure you both believe that. What you were exploring was the problem of how this love could remain a reality within a relationship that is presently marked by hostility and resentment. I'll try to deal with that question before the end of this letter.

"We don't seem to be compatible," you said. Who is? I have never found perfect compatibility in human relationships. A couple of sardines in a can are compatible, but you want more individuality than that! Someone has called mental incompatibility "nothing more than a case of carefully nurtured, garden-variety selfishness." That sounds a bit different, doesn't it? Incompatibility is so much kinder a word than selfishness.

Betty, do you remember how you said: "I can't stand being criticized by my husband?" Bill, you need to be more aware of your tendency to judge. It's a mark of self-centeredness also. An overly critical attitude will drive the other person away from you. It's true that with what measure we give, it will be measured to us again.

But why are you so upset about this criticism, Betty? Do you remember that you also added: "I can't stand being criticized, because I don't want him to have the last word." Why can't you stand for him to have the last word? Because *you* must have it? Isn't that selfishness, too?

In our conversation you raised the question on what the Bible teaches about divorce, and we did not take time to discuss this. I'm going to outline it for you, briefly. Because you were both brought up in the Christian faith and have always been taught that divorce is wrong, you now come face to face with an increasingly frustrating marital situation, and you don't know which way to turn.

You are certainly aware of the fact that all churches do not interpret the biblical teaching on divorce in the same manner. If they did it would be so easy. One church teaches no divorce, ever. Another may allow divorce, but no remarriage. Still other denominations allow divorce and remarriage for what they call "the innocent party." And there are Christians who permit divorce with remarriage for all who repent. So it goes. But it all must sound very puzzling. Who is right?

Jesus taught that marriage is a holy, beautiful, enduring relationship. He came into the world where men generally acted as they pleased without being ashamed or having a bad conscience. Rabbi Hillel had taught that a man could put away his wife for most any cause. And that was the accepted practice.

On one occasion the religious leaders approached Jesus with a question: "Is it lawful for a man to put away his wife for every cause" (Matt. 19:3)? If Jesus had replied that it was not lawful, the majority opinion would have been against him. The leaders knew that Jesus could not agree with loose divorce laws either. In answer Jesus turned to the opening chapters of Genesis. He pointed out that the two are one, and "whom therefore God has joined together, let no man put asunder" (Matt. 19:6).

Since they couldn't argue that, they returned with: "Then, why did Moses command to give a writing of divorce and put away the wife" (Matt. 19:7)? Such was the Mosaic law. If Moses permitted it, is this not reason enough for divorce?

Jesus answered: "Moses because of the hardness of your hearts suffered you to put away your wives: but from the beginning it was not so. And I say unto you, Whosoever shall put away his wife, except it be for fornication, and shall marry another commits adultery" (Matt. 19:8,9).

The ideal is no divorce. The plan of God from the beginning

was for union throughout a lifetime. True enough—the Scriptures allow two causes for divorce. Jesus speaks of fornication as one—a violation of trust, a breaking of this oneness, a betrayal of that relationship which God has established. Does this mean something physical only? Can there also be mental adultery? Spiritual unfaithfulness? Is it possible to be unfaithful in marriage through hostility and rebellion, resentment and critical judgments?

Of course I must add that adultery does not mean that divorce should follow automatically. Every sin can be forgiven, and in many a marriage such forgiveness of sin has led to a deeper love.

The other cause is willful desertion (see I Cor. 7:15). Suppose a husband deserts his wife and children. He runs off with another woman, lives with her and has more children. He does not return to his former wife. What should this Christian woman do? Legally she is still married. Should she obtain a divorce? Should she be penalized never to remarry?

Marriage is for life, but *for the hardness of your hearts* Jesus makes allowances. Do you not recognize this principle in the ministry of Jesus, in his merciful attitude toward the children of men? We must not see Jesus as a greater Pharisee than the Pharisees. They adhered strictly to the law. They were upset by Jesus as He kept breaking their regulations of cleanliness, separation and the sabbath. I see His life characterized by compassion, kindness, love, a deep understanding of human nature, the forgiveness of sins, and an acceptance of failure.

For Jesus, divorce was against the will of God, but He never rejected the divorcée. Nor did He keep anyone from the love of God. One of His longest conversations recorded in the New Testament took place with a woman who had been married five times and was then living with number six.

I would summarize Jesus' position this way: The law of God is strict, but the love of God is all-embracing. I take my clues from the life and teaching of Jesus, from all that He embodied, all that He did, and all that He presented as God in human flesh. I think that we must move beyond laws to the incarnation, the living out of the Father's love in mercy and compassion.

How, then, can you avoid a divorce? What can you do about your situation? That's the big question. Well, you will have to open up channels of communication to remove those hostilities and resentments. As the wife said to her husband hiding behind the newspaper at the breakfast table: "Pretend I'm a barber. Talk to me." The magazines and marriage columns are full of this type of advice.

Norman Vincent Peale suggests something more—a half hour experiment which he wants a couple to try for a week. During that half hour you project yourselves into the future as you consider what divorce will involve, what it will mean financially, emotionally, and to the children. You also recall the past and bring to remembrance happy memories. You consciously stop judging the other person during this half hour and turn critical eyes on yourself. "Unless you face up to the immaturities in yourself, unless you learn more about self-discipline and unselfishness than you have shown so far, you will probably find eventually (in case you divorce and marry someone else) that you have simply exchanged one set of emotional problems for another." (Taken from *Guideposts* Magazine, September 1964).

He also includes in his little experiment a time for meditation and prayer: "Be still and know that I am God" (Ps. 46:1). Betty, you said that Bill won't spend time with you for family devotions. And you asked how important it is for husbands and wives to pray together? Well, how important is it to do *anything* together? Isn't it of the utmost importance *now*? Would you therefore be willing to read and then meditate on that great chapter on love (I Corinthians 13) every night for a week? I have asked couples to do this before, and in some cases it has become the turning point for a better marriage.

That takes us back to the one question I have not answered yet. "We don't love each other any more." What is love? Is it something sentimental which you feel for someone who is good and worthy of love? But anyone can love another who is lovable. That is not yet Christian love. Christian love finds its pattern and origin in God. God loves us even though we are unlovable. God loves us in spite of the fact that we are undeserving. We haven't earned His love. We are unworthy. This love, expressed at the cross of Jesus, is agape-love, unmerited and free.

God's love proceeds spontaneously because it cannot help itself. It is not motivated by man's worthiness. It is entirely free and flows from itself. This is what we mean when we affirm that God is love.

As we open ourselves to this divine love, as we receive the love of God into our lives, we can become channels of that love to one another. And this means that we do not love another because of what we see in him or her. Rather, it is the very nature of love *to love*. You cannot rationalize this. You cannot explain it. If it is real, it must be both spontaneous and unmotivated.

Of course all this is easier said than done.

How do you suppose Jesus gained the power (as a man) to love those unlovable nobodies in Galilee and Jerusalem? And he loved them even to the point of death: "Christ died for the ungodly" (Rom. 5:6). From where did Jesus receive the love to love us as we are, when He knows everything about us? He loves us because He looks through our crust of sin, our degeneration, our unloveliness.

When we become aware to love in *this* light, Jesus himself will give us new eyes, new eyes to see one another as He sees us. Unworthy, yet worth dying for. Unlovely, yet loved to the point of death. Unacceptable, yet accepted. And this is how we love one another. I don't suppose it sounds quite right to point out for married people that we are to love even our enemies (although at times you may think of each other as enemies!). But how else can you love your enemies, unless you wake up to the realization that love is not extended to the worthy but to those who are totally undeserving? And "when we were enemies, we were reconciled..." (Rom. 5:10). That's how much Jesus loved us.

No, you are not Christ, but you are to be Christians—little Christs, followers of Jesus. And what else would it entail to live the Christian life?

Bill and Betty, don't give up your marriage, yet! You won't really gain anything by calling it quits. But if you are willing to persevere and live in this new love, you will discover that just as when you're driving in a tunnel, the way out is the way through.

Prayerfully and sincerely,

4

Letter to
a Teenager about
to Split

Dear Ted,

So you want to run away. You've had it up to here, and you can't take it any longer. O.K., but why did you want to tell me about it first? Isn't that an indication that you may not be quite so anxious to get free and do your thing? Maybe you still have your doubts. Maybe you don't really want to split.

Let me work on that assumption for a few moments. I'm only going to suggest that you read this with an open mind and then make your decision.

You know, Ted, as I look around at today's teens, they often seem to be talking tough, but they're not as tough as they talk. They may be compensating for some of the growing pains they're experiencing, working up courage. You know what compensating means? It's making up for something you lack, like the guy who feels inferior and turns into a loud mouth. So, you may really be afraid to split, and your fear is momentarily holding you back.

Haven't you discovered that many young people are constantly making excuses? (Older people too, of course.) They get to school late and they say, "I'm not late. They just started school before I got there." They go out for some sport, the ball doesn't bounce right and they're through. If studies are too hard, they fall behind and then drop out because they can't catch up.

It's always so much easier to make excuses for yourself than to shape up. So what if you don't make the football team? There are other sports. Try them. And what if you fail in all? Then there are achievements in science, mechanics, the arts. Giving up is so easy. Making excuses doesn't require any brains.

We've raised a whole generation by the permissive standards of Dr. Spock. The kids rebelling today are those babies who were picked up the moment they cried, and who never had much discipline. Everything came easy during a prosperous economy. As someone has said, their Spock marks are showing.

So, you're fed up with the school system, with education, with the society in which you're growing up, with our standards and goals. I don't blame you altogether. As a Christian there are many standards and goals in our American way of life against which we raise our voices too. Our education is often mere technological know-how for economic ends. We serve the twin gods of science and materialism. Jesus said that we cannot serve God *and* materialism. We cannot be loyal to two masters (Matt. 6:24). But you can see that we try to do it all the time.

And who wants the war? Or, how can we tolerate second-class citizenship for any minority? Yes, challenge the system. Challenge everything. But don't be impatient if the world doesn't change overnight at your commands. The trouble is that it's not likely to. But it's experiencing a lot of growing pains just now. There was this cartoon of a man being dragged off campus by a couple of bearded agitators, and he kept on insisting: "But I'm relevant, I tell you, I'm relevant!"

It's always simpler to cry out against the system than to change yourself! You want to change the world? Begin with yourself. The problem of the world is *your* problem. Do you hate anybody? Then how can you rage against war? Do you look down on anyone? Then how can you speak against inequality? Do you lust secretly—you wouldn't want anyone to know? Then how can you challenge values and morals?

Do you know the wisdom of the past? Then how can you discard it with a flip of the wrist? Has nothing been discovered in the history of man that is worth passing on? Wisdom didn't begin with you! I don't see that there is anything so terrible about standing on the shoulders of past generations. I myself am constantly amazed to discover that some of our present struggles were the same struggles and questions of the ancient Greeks! Anyway, you can't discard all this until you know what you're discarding.

Someone has said that when you're young you blame older people for all the troubles, and when you grow older the troubles are still there. Why? Because the trouble in the world is with man, not the other way around. It's not the world that's all wrong, but man. So, running away from home won't spell any concrete answers for you, Ted.

You're tired of parental authority. Understandable. I remember a mother who asked me: "When does a mother stop dictating to her daughter?" My first question to her was: "Why did you start to dictate?" And then: "Do you enjoy being a dictator?"

Maybe you believe that some parents do enjoy being dictators, but they have to be pretty warped in their minds to enjoy that role. Normal parents really don't want to be dictators. They want healthy relationships and understanding. Be thankful that some parents keep a tight rein. It shows their concern. If they didn't care, they wouldn't set any limits. Be grateful there are some limits being set for you.

Did you see that satirical picture of the generation gap? A

father says casually to his son about to go out for the evening: "Have a good time, son." The son replies: "Look, Dad, don't tell me what to do."

Another point. If you run away, aren't you giving in to pressures, rather than sticking up for principles? Aren't you capitulating to the group, the now way of life, the rebellious attitude, rather than charting your own course? And what do you accomplish? You merely exchange one type of bondage for another, if you want to call it that. What have you gained? The kids that run away say they are free, but are they? They wear the same way-out clothes, they all let their hair grow, they act carefree and lazy, they accept loose morals. They aren't actually that free. They're bound to another way of life in another social environment. And if you're bound, you're not free.

There was this girl who wrote to one of those Dear Abby columns: "I am interested in being a nice girl and well thought of, but not, of course, if it's going to interfere with my popularity." Was she free? Or was she bound to some concept of popularity, which would actually dictate a new morality to her? (I'm using the word 'dictate' deliberately.) That's the scene.

I want to tell you about a man who was very much tempted to run away. It was a different time, but what we're discussing turns out to be similar. His name was Nehemiah. He lived during a period when his people Israel had been vanquished and taken captive by the Babylonians. Jerusalem lay in ruins. For a generation it lay in ruins. Then the Israelites wanted to return to their land, and they received permission to come back.

When Nehemiah saw the city like that, he felt called to do one thing—to build the wall, to construct the gate, to make Jerusalem safe again. He started in immediately.

But there were enemies who didn't like what was happening. They ridiculed Nehemiah and laughed at his efforts. When this did not perturb old Nehemiah, they tried to infiltrate his labor force. But they failed. Then they started a war of nerves. They were going to stop him. Would Nehemiah attend a discussion? He would not. Would he come to their towns and meet with them? There was nothing to talk about. They harassed him, annoyed him, hired false prophets to threaten him, but Nehemiah continued with his assignment. He prayed. Finally he answered his enemies: "Should such a man as I flee? (Neh. 6:11) Should I run away? Why?"

From what would he run away? He had a job to do, a wall to build. Should he leave it unfinished? You have an education to complete, your preparation for life to finish. Why should you run out on it?

Jesus told a story of a man who began to build but was not able to finish. He started to construct a tower, but he ran out of funds. Everyone walked by his unfinished project, remarking: "Look at that! This fellow began to build but was not able to finish" (See Luke 14:28-30).

I'm afraid that this applies to those who have left their families, forsaken their education and would not complete what they started. Often they turn out to be pitiful, immature adults who continue to run away from problems and never reach their goals. And you can't imagine the nagging regrets, the inner frustrations and the painful sense of failure which keep tugging away at their usefulness and vitality.

And, to what would you flee? Some escape to the city and others to the country. Some escape to the suburbs and others to apartments. Where would you go? The trouble with some people is that they started to run in their teens and they've never stopped. They're always running scared, always evading responsibility, and always disappointed in themselves!

How would you like to live by this philosophy: "The best that man can hope and strive and pray for is momentary happiness during life, repeated as frequently as the cards allow. To me pleasure and my personal happiness are all I deem worth a hoot."

Can you see, Ted, that this statement contains pessimistic

undertones? This man cannot cope with frustration and dissatisfaction. He must escape. He seeks endless rounds of pleasure, but he does not seem to find happiness his way. He has probably discovered how empty it all is, but he keeps up his frantic pursuit.

Well, how can you meet this problem? First off, you'll have to face the issue, square off against it. Like Nehemiah. The great psychiatrist Carl Jung said that this is the most difficult part of life—to face a situation, not to make excuses, not to run away, but honestly to examine your own life. Do you want to be honest about it? Then first of all, Ted, you will have to face yourself.

Do you know the difference between a team and a gang? A team is where you can prove your courage on your own and contribute to others. A gang is a place you go to hide. A gang is the scene where adults can't get any information about you, but it doesn't prove a thing. Those who are hiding out have only changed their scene, not themselves.

Then you will also have to fight the problem. While Nehemiah was continually harassed, he battled his temptations. That's why the New Testament tells us to put on the whole armor of God. Why? So that we may be protected and able to stand against the enemy. How? Well, that spiritual armor includes truth and righteousness, salvation and the Word of God, inner peace and faith in Christ. We wrestle not against the world itself, but against the powers behind this world. There's a spiritual warfare going on against the forces which drive men to be hateful, destructive, corrupt.

That's a point which modern young people have largely overlooked. The battle is not only with a corrupt system, it is against demonic forces which inspire these systems. To use more biblical language, these demons must be cast out in order that man may be saved and serve the true God. Serve Him in sincerity and truth. (You'll find this warfare spelled out in Ephesians 6.)

"Saints are the sinners who keep on trying," wrote Robert Louis Stevenson. Right? Not giving up but going on. Facing their disillusionment, fighting their battles, and therefore winning their victories. If you're tempted to run away, why not ask yourself as Nehemiah did whether a person like you should run? I don't care how many others may want you to split, but why should *you*? What's in it for you, after all? You don't have to be like them. You can be yourself!

Before you make any decision take a good, hard look down both roads which stretch out before you. You're at the intersection now!

There'll be a broader way which looks easy. You can't really tell the cost because it's so much like our credit system—nothing down and thirty-six easy payments, beginning next year. (Whoever kidded us into believing that any of the payments would be *easy*?) The other road will be narrower and more demanding. You can tell even now that it will cost you some commitment.

"We are more than conquerors through him that loved us," wrote Paul (Rom. 8:37). But how can anyone become *more* than a conqueror when he makes excuses or runs away from responsible living?

So I hope, Ted, that you won't take that easy road where you can shift yourself into neutral and coast downhill until you bang up against hell's iron gate. The narrow way leads upward. It's hard. It demands discipline, effort, dedication. It winds all about the mountain, but in spite of its hardness it will bring you to the view at the top, and eternal life.

What do you really want out of life, Ted?

Sincerely,

37

5

Letter to
Parents Whose Son
Was Killed in the War

Dear Jim and Ellen,

I wish it were possible to write some magic words that would make all your sorrow vanish, but how can anyone be sufficient for that? When you shared with me the sad news about Gary, it almost seemed as if you were hoping for a miracle. But who can ever really forget the loss of a son? And when you think back over the long history of the world which has seen far more wars than peace, you arrive at the stark realization that this human heartbreak has occurred over and over again, on our side as well as on the enemy's. We're never just killing soldiers, guerrillas or troops, but sons and husbands and sweethearts, members of the human family, boys who are loved. What a hellish business is war!

I'm trying to place myself in your shoes, to feel the hurt, the emptiness, the suffering, although I'm not actually called on to join your experience. Death is always sad news, and especially a violent death such as this one. Gary was such a fine, gifted, handsome young man—surely headed for a good life. Perhaps all I can say is that I share deeply in your sorrow and loss.

Now, isn't it a fact that the more you love anyone, the greater the pain you feel? If you don't care very much about some object, it doesn't matter whether that dish breaks or a vase shatters on the floor. But if it's your favorite piece from your prize collection. . . ? Surely, there is no comparison whatsoever between a material object and your son.

Does this mean the answer is not to get involved in life, not to love? Of course not. You expect a risk in love, in getting caught up in living, in having children. We keep on accepting these risks, because that's the way we want to live.

Ellen, you wrote that you have been almost numb for a month now; in a state of shock. Jim seems to be accepting it more calmly, but I'm sure that he is experiencing the pangs of emptiness too. You have poured the greatest part of your lives into your children, and now it's all gone. Lost! And, in spite of the fact that you love your other children, no one could (or should) replace Gary.

Your friends have been a great source of comfort to you. We certainly learn how many friends we have in times like these. Yet the burden remains. I am glad that you have not turned bitter about this, but you are filled with questions. There is nothing wrong with asking why! It is only natural. No one in his right mind would pass through a crisis like this without asking why.

Let me refer you to the book of Job. In the first two chapters we are told of his great tragedies. He loses all of his possessions and his family, children and grandchildren, in one fatal stroke. In chapter three he begins to question. And he does not stop until the end of the book, until he is accorded a vision of God.

You have no doubt been reminded of the fact that Gary is with God. He has entered into eternity and inherited the biblical promises. We believe that in heaven we shall see one another again. There is surely comfort in this revelation, since we know that all sorrow and suffering, all pain and death will cease. But the tone of your letter is more immediate.

Something else is at stake—your concept of God. You wrote: "I feel I can't accept this. It's just too big a burden." And, "we all have accepted this as God's will." Now, Ellen, if you accept it as God's will, and yet carry a burden of not accepting it, what is your concept of God? How do you picture Him? As good or bad? As a cold Sovereign or as a heavenly Father? Is He concerned about you or not?

Let me put it this way. In a sense what has taken place is *not* the will of God. I mean, war is not the will of God, sin is not the will of God, and so death is not the will of God. All this is allowed in this evil world in which we live, but it is not His perfect will. God allows wars because man has become greedy, sinful, selfish and rebellious. But on the other hand, God is not responsible for it, just as He is not responsible when an alcoholic plows his car into an innocent child.

God has given us freedom. We are responsible. We misuse that freedom. We are free to love and experience the risks of that love, as I said a moment ago. We are also free not to love, not to risk, and therefore to grow cold, hard, careless and selfish. Such is our freedom, to drink or not to drink, to make war or not to make war, to love or not to love, to believe or not to believe, to accept or not to accept the comfort of God.

One month after his son was killed by a murderer who was never apprehended, killed while sitting at his desk in his study, Dr. Robert Speer, a great missionary leader wrote to a friend: "I do not believe for a moment that wrongs like this are a part of the will of God. They must grieve God far more than they can grieve man, but our comfort is that God's love sets to work to do all that the love of God can do to atone for such evil. All this one reads in the cross where the murder of God's Son has been made the redemption of mankind." He had earlier confessed that he could not understand it at all. He could only trust infinite wisdom and love.

Do you grasp what he was saying about the will of God? I

don't like to hear people blandly dismiss everything with the pious phrase: "It's the will of God." That is a judgment which they make on a situation. And it sounds like a very holy judgment. But I can only discover the will of God in any situation for myself. I can never say to you that it was the will of God that Gary should die so young. What comfort would there be in that? It only raises more questions. If later (perhaps much later) you yourselves can see some purpose, well and good. But that is for you to discover, and not for me to pontificate.

Here is another thought that sometimes enters our minds. "Why did this happen to me? What did I do to deserve this?" I have a simple answer to such questions—nothing, absolutely nothing. Of course we always have regrets in our lives. We would have done something differently, and we feel guilty about our past. Then the thought of punishment for wrongs suddenly arises when tragedy strikes. And we say to ourselves that we understand why that happened. We are being punished.

How wrong we are. Is it fair to think that another life is being used to punish you? You wouldn't dream of doing this to anyone else, so why should we charge our heavenly Father with punishing us in this round about manner? As I said, our whole concept of God is at stake. I won't accept for a moment the thought that punishment is in this tragedy.

All this has happened under the eyes of God, who sees every sparrow that falls to the ground. True. But who is this God who allows human suffering? Is this not the God and Father of our Lord Jesus Christ, who has come into the world for our sins? Does not Jesus Himself reveal this loving Father? Is not His life of poverty, His birth in a stable, His death on a cross the supreme expression of God's love for man?

God is our heavenly Father. Our heavenly Father had only one Son, and He allowed Him to be killed and put to death for us. And this implies that the eternal God has felt even more deeply than we ever could the emptiness, loneliness and loss of His only beloved.

We have agreed, haven't we, that the greater the love, the greater the suffering? And if God is love, perfect love, can we possibly imagine the pain which He endured at the cross of Jesus? Can we humans even approach the extent of this love? Salvador Dali has a painting of the crucifixion in which you view the cross from above. That is, you are looking down on the bowed head and shoulders of Jesus. You cannot see his face. And this crucified figure is set against the most dense, black background. But using this unusual perspective, the artist has pictured the greatness of *God's sorrow* at the death of his Son.

Now, if this is how you view God, if this is how you think of the heavenly Father to whom you pray, if this is how you receive the good news of Jesus, a ray of sunshine will break through the gathering clouds. And that is not make believe. Life can spring up even from the most terrible cross. It did years ago. And it still does. The cross brings faith, hope and salvation to many.

Therefore let me change your question from a *why* to *how*. You will never fully know why you are called upon to carry this terrible burden, but everything will depend on how you carry it. What will this do to you? What will it make of you?

When tragedy strikes, some people lose their faith (whatever faith they had). Was it faith in a God who would protect them from all sorrow and tragedy? But other people begin to consider how they can cope with this. They know they have to. They never will forget their loss, but somehow or other a new dimension is added to their lives.

Another man and his wife lost their only son while he was in the service. He was driving home one night with his buddy at the wheel. His buddy fell asleep. They crashed. His buddy survived, but he died instantly. He was eighteen. They still speak of their only son with tears in their eyes, but in spite of their irreplacable loss, they are living in faith.

You will discover another fact. Your real growth in life comes through tests and trials. During these experiences you begin to think about the meaning and purpose of life, things we neglect too often while we're on the merry-go-round of our daily tasks. You will be drawn to God Himself through your trials.

So, let me suggest that you read a little from the book of Job. Then turn to the life of Jesus. Consider His love for people, His compassion for the individual, His dedication to give Himself freely for our sins.

Romans 8 is also helpful: "If God be for us who can be against us?" God spared not His only Son for us all. He has demonstrated His fatherly love toward us. So He promises not to withhold anything from us. Yes, we may suffer, we may be persecuted, we may go through the valley. We may even be "killed all the day long," but we may have the assurance through it all that nothing in life or death will separate us from the love of God which is in Jesus Christ our Lord.

Dear Jim and Ellen, I have attempted to share your sorrow in this delicate and difficult time. Please receive my words in the spirit with which they are written. And may the Word of God bring healing and hope into your lives, so that you will walk through the valley with the knowledge that the mountains are not far away.

He who died for us also rose again!

With warm regards,

Letters about Personal Problems

"A scorner seeketh wisdom, and findeth it not:
but knowledge is easy unto
him that understandeth."

Prov. 14:6

6

Letter to
a Girl Who
Can't Say No

Dear Janet,

Let me begin by telling you how very much I appreciated your forthright letter. You were honest and direct, and I know it was not easy for you to bring your problem out into the open. But now you are no longer willing to bury it, since it's beginning to fester in your subconscious.

I've given your question much thought, Janet, but I must make one preliminary observation. It's extremely difficult to write about any matter such as yours and actually get to the root through correspondence. We are complex beings. Psychiatry has taught us that there are no quick solutions. Therefore I do suggest that it may become necessary for you to talk to a specialist. I hope you understand why I am saying this. We may not be able to dig things out completely like this. Even so I'm not saying that you must seek counseling, but that it *may* prove to be helpful.

With this word of caution I'll get to the matter at hand. It is only natural that we want members of the opposite sex to be attracted to us. Most normal people want to be accepted, liked and sometimes admired. At least appreciated. The problem arises when this desire for attention gets out of hand. You're afraid it's beginning to in your case. You like to attract men, physically. You know you shouldn't think this way, but you feel some excitement about it. As you say, it seems exciting to be bad.

Of course it does. Evil must be alluring, or else who would be interested? Why is there a perfume called "My Sin"? Because it sounds so intriguing, that's why. The forbidden is constantly glamorized and evil is made fascinating. We really believe that we can have a good time being bad. That's a twist, isn't it? How can you have a *good* time being *bad*? (I suppose some people think you have a bad time being good!) But if I know anything about the English language, that doesn't make sense.

Janet, you remind me of one of the girls in the musical *Oklahoma*. She sings a catchy little ditty called, "I'm just a girl who can't say no." One of the stanzas sounds like this: "I'm just a girl who can't say no, I'm in a terrible fix. I always say 'come on, let's go', just when I ought to say nix."

What if you can't say no? What's a person to do? You know right from wrong, but you can't bring yourself to do the right. Now, that's a very human dilemma.

I will admit that there are times when you can't say no. When you get too close to a fire, you will be burned. Nobody can save you when you get within ten yards of Niagara Falls. But give yourself more room and you have a chance. When you allow a fellow to have too much freedom with your body, you may not be able to stop each other. But establish some boundaries previously, and you can call it to a halt. If you're honest about it, you will admit that you can say *no* from a safe distance.

But what if you have already talked yourself into that frame of mind where you want to say *yes?* You've decided that there's no need to hold back. That's a horse of a different color. But now look what's happened: you're no longer at the place where you can't say no, you just don't want to! The song from *Oklahoma* actually gives the wrong impression. It shouldn't have been, "I'm just a girl who can't say no." It ought to have been, "I'm just a girl who *won't* say no."

And that raises another question. Why not? Why won't you say no? What is buried so deeply within that allows you to play along with that permissive element of our society? What are your real drives and needs? This is where a psychiatrist may be of help. He may uncover some inner mechanism that triggers your emotional needs to seek some fulfillment.

I could also ask you some questions: Did you feel accepted as a child? Loved by your mother? What of your father? Do you feel very secure now? Do you feel accepted by God? By people? Do you accept yourself? My guess would be that you come up pretty negative on some of those questions, and because you feel so insecure (for whatever reasons) you are eager to assert your femininity.

Here's an illustration. A playboy is really out to prove his masculinity through his conquests. If he were certain of himself, he wouldn't have to run from one girl to the next. The professional stripper or go-go girl may in some cases be after a fast buck, but what she really wants is to have men ogle her and perhaps lust. Why? Because she is rather insecure. She may even feel unworthy, and she wants to prove that she can create some excitement around her.

Or, consider what the experts say about most of the professional football players. They must prove to themselves that they are really men. In spite of their muscle and meat, they often remain unsure.

What are *you* trying to prove? And why? If you had the inner conviction that you are loved and accepted *as you are,* you wouldn't have to make it be known that you're a girl who won't say no.

Explore those questions. Face yourself. Don't be afraid to. No, it's not easy. It's far more comfortable to continue in your established patterns, than to turn about and face those insecurities. But since you've written about your inordinate desires, this is the only way to begin.

Now suppose you discover what has contributed to your insecurities. How can you become more secure? That's the question. If insecurity is the cause of your running amuck, what can you do to change that? The answer to this question will alter your behavior.

Now I want to put it to you straight, Janet. I believe that there is no greater knowledge of security than that which is found in the gospel of Jesus Christ. "To all who did receive him, to those who have yielded him their allegiance, he gave the right to become children of God" (John 1:12, NEB). If you will accept the fact that God loves you, that Christ has given Himself for you, and that you can become a child of God by faith in Him, you will take the biggest step of your life toward inner stability. If you can receive this good news, you will know that you are accepted by Him.

The word of Jesus is that if you receive Him, you are a child of God. And if you believe that you are a child of God, then you are loved, then you are accepted. You have that right! It is not only you who accept Jesus Christ. God accepts you. He receives you into His family.

It may be too late to do anything about the acceptance you missed because your parents didn't give it sufficiently. It may be too late to change what was lacking in your formative years. But it is never too late to bask in the acceptance that comes through Jesus Christ. It is the only antidote to insecurity. And like a fresh coat of paint which covers the old stains and imperfections, so a healing influence will spread over your whole existence.

How can you be sure? You can only believe Jesus. Do you? He has come from God. He tells it to us as it is. As long as you

50

are unable to put your faith in Christ and give Him your allegiance, you will frantically grasp for acceptance whenever and wherever you can. Even in ways you may later regret. But that leads to frustration and feelings of unworthiness. So the place to begin is to turn to God. Not as an extra. Not for a diversion, but for the security that comes as a child of God.

Janet, you will also need to feel more accepted by people, people through whom the love of God is embodied. And that's where the Christian church comes in, for that's what the church should be all about—a family of those who believe, a fellowship of those who are children of God, and therefore brothers and sisters of one another. Find a small group of Christians. Share your faith with them. You will learn that they are very much like you. They have their problems too. And they are learning to cope with them.

If you don't feel worthy of their company, just realize that we are all in the same boat. We are all unworthy. All of us. And yet Jesus died for us. He was willing to sacrifice Himself on the cross in our behalf. And that means we were worth dying for, worth redeeming. Just look at the cross. It's the clue to faith and fellowship.

I must now turn to another related question in your letter. You write: "I don't know what I'm trying to prove." That's an interesting insight. You're aware that you're trying to prove something, but suppose you were sure of something. Would you need to prove it?

Think for a moment about the temptation of Jesus in the wilderness. (You will find this recorded in Matt. 4:1-11.) The tempter said to Him: "If you are the Son of God. . ." That should be translated: "*Since* you are the Son of God. . ." What the tempter was raising as a question was simply: "Are you what you say you are? Are you sure you are the Son of God? Shouldn't you prove it to yourself? Then turn these stones into bread and prove that you are what you think you are. . ."

Jesus did not need to prove anything to Himself: "Man shall

51

not live by bread alone, but by every word that proceeds from the mouth of God." He was already certain. He lived in another dimension. He lived by the Word of God. There was nothing to prove.

Janet, if you don't have to prove to yourself that you are beautiful or sexually desirable, don't you see what a liberating effect this will have on you? You'll be free! And you won't let yourself give in to men, nor will you seek to attract them all the time.

And that raises another point. Jesus resisted the devil. He taught us self discipline. "Take up the cross," He said. He called us to follow Him, to deny ourselves, and even to pluck out our eyes if they led us astray, or cut off our hands if they offended us. He talked about this in connection with the very question you have raised—lust.

Of course He did not intend that we were literally to cut off our hands or gouge out our eyes. (If that was to be interpreted literally, few of us would keep any of our members.) He meant that we become serious Christians, earnest and disciplined, to remove those desires which arise from within. And since we may treasure our temptations as much as we treasure an eye or a hand, they will not be so easy to tear out.

You know how much simpler it is to sing, "I can't say no." How tough to put it the other way: "I won't say no." It is so much easier to make excuses than to offer resistance; to turn from evil means effort and struggle. But it's the only road to inner peace, the only road to overcoming those sickening guilt feelings.

One final thing. The apostle Paul allowed us to look into his inner struggles in such a realistic, open way that it was like turning on the light in a very dark room. He knew the raging battle between good and evil, but he also experienced the freedom and power which came through surrender to Christ. In all honesty he wrote:

"My own behavior baffles me. I find myself not doing what

I really want to do but doing what I really loathe. . . I often find that I have the will to do good, but not the power. That is, I don't accomplish the good I set out to do, and the evil I don't really want to do I find I am always doing. . . In my mind I am God's willing servant, but in my own nature I am bound fast, as I say, to the law of sin and death. It is an agonizing situation, and who on earth can set me free from the clutches of my own sinful nature? I thank God there *is* a way out through Jesus Christ our Lord" (Rom. 7:15-25, Phillips).

There are no easy recipes for victory. But if you're just a girl who won't say no, at least examine that premise. You can find security in yielding to the love of God in Jesus Christ. You have the right to be called a child of God, loved and accepted. While many Christians urge you to accept Christ, just realize that the Bible teaches us that *God in Christ accepts you*! He really does. Just as you are. That's the good news. It's actually true—you are forgiven at the cross, and you are accepted.

In that new certainty you can live with assurance and freedom. So may the love of God and the grace of Jesus Christ be with you!

7

Letter to a Playboy

Dear Jack,

I don't really know why you wrote to me, unless it was simply a challenge to feel me out on the subject of sex. You surely stated your bold position forcefully, and in a way you are asking for some sort of rebuttal (if there is any) to the Playboy Philosophy.

"What's wrong with sex?" you ask. Nothing. God made it, and it's a beautiful expression of love and oneness. But man has a way of degrading everything he touches, and he can make sex ugly and cheap. Man has a way of doing that because of what we Christians call the fall. Incidentally, the French existentialist Albert Camus wrote a book entitled *The Fall*, which is a modern interpretation of man's egocentricities and self-destructiveness.

"What's the church got against an unmarried fellow having a good time?" you ask. "Besides, we men are made the way we are, and you can't go against human nature." And yet you also admit to a conflict with what you understand to be the

Christian way of life. You admit such an outlook is only out for number one, and it doesn't take into consideration that the other person may get hurt. And a girl may become pregnant, may be forced into an abortion, and more seriously may be damaged inwardly by excessive guilt.

All this has been discussed, yes almost beaten to death, in our frank society, so I'm not about to rehash those same old arguments. But you did make one passing remark about something that's troubling you. You don't like the way you're beginning to think about girls. You've lost your respect for women, even the entire human race. You wonder whether there is any decency anywhere, and you don't like what this is doing to your thinking.

Now I'd like to enter that door which you've opened for me and ask you a question. My question may seem to be, at first, beside the point. But I'm coming around to the issue you raise, if you will hear me out.

Here's my question: "If I were to tell you a dirty story, would you listen?" Nine chances out of ten, you would. Perhaps some would excuse themselves, but aren't most people interested in something that may be a bit suggestive? It seems to me that our society is increasingly moving in bolder directions.

There's hardly a play on Broadway that does not contain coarse jokes and suggestive remarks. They shut down one play the other day that portrayed every conceivable sort of sex play on stage. The point is not that they shut it down. The inconceivable part is that such a play was even produced!

Novels won't sell unless they contain offensive material and utterly frank descriptions which may border on catering to prurient interests. You can't pass a newsstand or magazine rack without encountering sensual and risque material. And I'm not now talking about the hardcore pornography which is sold under cover.

Need I mention the majority of motion pictures which

portray a freedom of expression undreamed of a few years ago? And some college periodicals delight in printing all the obscene words which you formerly encountered only in public toilets.

One morning my seven-year-old daughter asked me: "Daddy, do you know the story of Alice in Wonderland?" (I told her I did.) Later that day I drove past a movie theater with a mod picture title: "Alice in Acidland." And I wondered what happens to us in that short span of innocence at seven to excursions at seventeen?

Now my next question is, why? Why is this so? Why are we dirty-minded? Why do we move from one suggestive piece to the next? Is this simply the trend of the times, or does it betray something more fundamental in human nature? I think that's really the case.

We may consider all this suave, sophisticated, avant-garde, the smart new society. Everything is out in the open. Yet somehow it's beginning to stink like garbage that was allowed to stand around on the streets of New York during a strike. What a stench. A smart new society must learn that smart has never yet been spelled s-m-u-t.

But, Jack, consider also the other side of our nature. We lean in the opposite direction, because we want things to be clean, washed, polished. Do you enjoy driving around in a dirty car? Probably not. You don't even want your windshield dirty, and you complain when they don't wipe it clean every time you stop for gas. And what about all that refuse and paper in city streets? We even have to campaign with the slogan that "every litter-bit hurts."

Do you enjoy wearing a shirt that is soiled around the collar? When you enter a house do you like to see the dust so thick that you can write your initials on the table? What is your impression of a home where things are strewn about helter skelter, and everything is always in a mess? Have you noticed how generally the people who live in this manner are mixed up too? Their very surroundings proclaim their confusion.

That's the point. Instinctively we want cleanliness and order. Then, what about our minds? Why are we not as meticulous there? Why are we willing to wash the outside but leave the inside dirty?

Now, Jack, if you're still with me until I get around to your remarks about sex, let's take another step forward. Isn't it a fact that the more you contact the good, the true and the pure, the more you shun the impure, the suggestive, the lewd? And conversely, isn't it also true that the more you give yourself over to the coarse, the vulgar and the off-beat, the less you will consider anything wrong, the less you will fail to recognize plain dirt?

Some people do not consider much of anything offensive any more. Even some Christians will give you an argument for the most rabid forms of art, literature, drama and motion pictures. Others have lowered their squirming point so far that they can sit through a performance without any twinge of conscience. They have ceased to be shocked at the indecent, the frankly degrading, or the bold, crass displays of sensuality. To those people who have anaesthetized their conscience there is, of course, very little more to say.

But I started out with a question and it should be answered. Why do we have a bent in our character toward the suggestive, to more and more lurid forms of entertainment? Obviously, far too many people in our society are making a fast buck simply because of that evil bent in our nature!

So let me give you a straight answer. Dirty-mindedness is a symptom of something deeper. What is actually the matter with man is that he is a sinner. (That should be rather obvious by now; I won't have to belabor the point.) Therefore, since man is a sinner he can become dirty-minded. Not the other way around! *Because* he is a sinner, he goes in for perversions of the true, the good, the beautiful.

Once you grasp this fact you come to the root of the trouble, to the disease itself. And then you will refuse to deal with the symptoms. Confront man in his inherent sinfulness, and as a result "sins" may begin to vanish. Cut out the disease, and the symptoms will disappear.

Do you begin to see now why I have taken this excursion, why I did not give you the usual answers for the current Playboy Philosophy? It's not the philosophy that's on trial. The real trouble lies deeper. War is not the issue, but what makes men war? Racial inequalities are not to blame but why do we not love our neighbor as ourselves? Why do we in our homes hurt, destroy and degrade one another until there is nothing left but to divorce? The fundamental problem is with man himself—diseased, sick, infected with egocentricity which may border on egomania. The Bible calls it sin.

And once you recognize this, Jack, your perspective changes. The question is no longer *why* but *how*? How do you overcome not only sensuality and dirty-mindedness, but more important, how do you overcome this basic defect in humanity? How do you operate on the disease itself?

The first answer is obvious: Do you really want to change? Do you want to do something about it? Are you willing? If you are not, are you at least willing to be made willing? Willing to think about truth, justice, mercy, purity, love? Willing to think about God, Christ, the coming judgment, eternity, and the love of God for a world gone astray?

Let me assume that you are willing. Now what? Shun the evil, the lewd, the vulgar. Avoid them like the plague. Make contact with the pure, the honest, the Christian. Evil is overcome by good!

All this may help outwardly, but within you the same seething desires are still burning. The flames of the volcano have not been extinguished. Something more is needed, but what?

Go back to our illustration about cleanliness. We want clean cars, shirts, homes, streets. How do you get your car clean? You have it washed. How about your shirts? You throw them into the machine or take them to the laundry. How does a house get clean? It's vacuumed, dusted, polished. To wash a car, clean clothes, dust the house, sweep the streets *someone else or something else besides the object being cleaned has to do it.* The car, house or street never clean themselves.

So, likewise, we human beings cannot change ourselves. We need our minds washed, our thoughts cleansed, our hearts purified. Therefore the Bible says: "According to his mercy he saved us, by the washing of regeneration, and renewing of the Holy Ghost" (Titus 3:5). God washes us—our minds, our hearts, our lives. It is something that is done for us.

Or again, in the Gospels Jesus says to His disciples: "You have already been cleansed by the word that I spoke to you" (John 15:3 NEB). He speaks the word that makes us clean. He alone can renew us.

Jesus began to wash the disciples' feet around the table during the night of the last supper. Peter objected. He didn't want Jesus to wash *his* feet. Jesus replied that if Peter was not willing to subject himself to washing, He would have no part with him. The impulsive Peter immediately asked Jesus to wash his entire body. Jesus replied that he was clean, except for his feet.

What did this mean? Peter was clean and washed and forgiven because he was a Christian. He had been fully accepted by Jesus. But in his regular, daily life he was in need of continual washing. The feet were a symbol of that which in daily contacts becomes soiled.

Do you see this other truth? Peter *was* washed and clean and accepted. Something had been done for him, something had happened to him— the washing of regeneration, the word of renewal through the Spirit of God.

So, Jack, I'm not about to argue about the Playboy Philosophy. What I'm really after is something else. Your whole outlook on life! What are you living for? Where are you going—ultimately? Are you a Christian? The way you think about girls is only a part of the larger question whether you are self-centered or God-centered? Egocentric or committed to Christ? All out for number one, or do you love your neighbor as a person?

If you still feel that I've brushed your question aside, I'm sorry, because I didn't mean to do that. I've actually attempted to take you from the shallow waters to the area where you can do some swimming about. The main point: "What does a man gain by winning the whole world at the cost of his true self? What can he give to buy that self back?" (Mark 8:36,37, NEB).

Those are the stakes. Everything else is just peanuts. Think about it. I'm sure you will.

Yours,

8

Letter to an Alcoholic

Dear Bob,

So you finally admit that you have a drinking problem. Now that you've said it, we can talk. Up till now you always used to kid me that you could give it up any time you liked, but, of course, you never liked.

Let's get straight to your big question. What do you do now? How can you stop drinking? How can you overcome your problem? And even more specifically, as you put it, how can I make myself find a new way of life? Let me try to offer some answers.

Basically you have what I might call a want-to problem. That's very human. You admit that you are in all probability an alcoholic, or at least that you could very well become addicted, even though you find it hard to call yourself one. Any habit such as this turns into a want-to problem, into a matter of the will. Not that will power is everything, or that you can do anything you like if you make enough resolutions. That's not true. But we have to start somewhere.

I've been trying to teach my son that he must want to learn. I cannot push him into studying. Not forever. It will have to come from within him. He has a good head on his shoulders, and if he will apply himself he can go places. But if he does not want to, he squanders those God-given brains. And if he refuses to apply himself while he is young, he may regret it later on.

But you have a different situation. Your want-to area is defective. You've drugged yourself with alcohol. It's become a habit. And that means you will find it more difficult to muster your resolves or turn your will about. This may begin to sound to you as if you need medical attention, and surely there may be some help for you medically. But when you sober up a little, you have to ask yourself what you really want out of life. And that's where your will comes in.

Therefore I'd like you to ask yourself some pretty rough questions. Are you ready? O.K.

"Do I want to be happy or do I like to suffer?" I mean that. Ask yourself whether you like playing the role of a martyr.

"Do I want the real things out of life, or do I enjoy faking it? Do I want freedom which comes with sobriety, or do I want to continually escape from reality? Do I want a home and wife and children, or am I willing to end up some day without anything—in the gutter?"

I know there are men who begin to drown their sorrows when they lose a wife or family. It may be some unforeseen tragedy that actually sets them off. But that is a false conclusion! The tragedy and suffering is not responsible for a man becoming a bum. Such a man had nothing much to live for *before* the tragedy struck. He probably had no other goals besides his family, home and job. And, as you know, we need more than that. Jesus told us to seek first the kingdom of God. That's sound advice.

I suppose these questions about losing your family are a little too forceful because you're not facing those problems yet.

But if you continue in your present direction, who knows? You have a faithful wife. She's stuck by you. But she may not always. She's been troubled about your behavior in front of the children, when you're home, that is.

Don't think I'm trying to scare you with these hard questions, but I want to tell you about the chaplain who told me a pathetic story about a man in jail. That man had had a few beers and on his way home ran down a child he didn't see in front of his car. Can you identify with his guilt?

That sounds rather extreme, I know, but you are aware of the fact that alcohol plays a role in a very high percentage of accidents. Hasn't Alice warned you many times that she's scared when you're driving under the influence? Not only scared for you, but for what you may do behind the wheel. You're not fit to handle a car, and yet until now you've been spared.

So, what do you want, Bob? The freedom of sobriety or a phony escape from reality? Let me be honest: As long as you keep on drinking you really *want to* drink more than anything else. And that means you're still running scared.

Now comes the next question: Why are you running away? What are you afraid of? What can't you face? Something in your business? You don't like your work? People don't recognize your abilities? You're not advancing as fast as you hoped? You sometimes wonder whether you're over the hill, now that you've discovered the beginnings of that bald spot on top? Are you disappointed with yourself? Are you beginning to realize that all your dreams will not be realized? That's quite a shock!

Or are you disgusted with your home life? Your family? Your children are not growing up as you expected they would? You can't make them turn into the persons you hoped them to become? And do you harbor any hostility toward Alice? Why? Are you simply frustrated with life? The rat race? The heavy traffic? Or just plain bored? Bored stiff?

63

Why do you drink? For once, Bob, don't rationalize this one away. Face it. You see, yours is not a medical problem but a moral one. You've been sold a bill of goods which you know you shouldn't have bought. So, what's really playing on the screen of your life? Some escapist, humorous comedy? Some song and dance routine on a meaningless merry-go-round? Some Western that reminds you of the good old days? Or a heavy tragedy which no one can seem to resolve? What's playing?

Now let me suggest another avenue of thought. Your drinking has become habitual. Any habit, this or any other, must be thought of as a chain. It becomes a very strong chain because of the past, and it holds you in its clutches. Still it's a chain, constructed one link at a time. *Today* is the link between yesterday and tomorrow.

If, therefore, you can break today's link with the past and the future, you've broken the habit. By breaking today's link you free yourself from the past and can begin to face the future. Once you accomplish this, it's important to realize that you don't have to worry about the next day or the next or the next. That's all you need to do!

So if you're going to quit, *quit.* Just like that. Break the chain of habit. And when tomorrow arrives it will be easier to do the same, since you already made the resolve today. And the longer you manage to keep it up, the stronger your new chain will become—the chain of good habits.

But, Bob, I do realize that all I've said so far is only preparatory. The next step is the big one. You have written to me, a minister, because you probably believed that since you couldn't handle your problem, there may be help from another source. From God. You're right.

One of the most experienced organizations in this field of alcoholism has discoverd the same truth. Alcoholics Anonymous has a program of twelve steps. First they admit that they are powerless over alcohol and then they confess: "We came to believe that a Power greater than ourselves could restore us to sanity, and made a decision to turn our will and our lives over to the care of God as we understood Him." (Steps two and three.)

Since you believe in God, you will only find difficulty in surrendering yourself, committing yourself to this living Lord. "The crisis of self-surrender has always been and must always be regarded as the vital turning point of the religious life, " wrote William James. But we cannot convert ourselves.

That's why Jesus had to come. If we could have saved ourselves and made ourselves fit for God, we would not have needed His coming, His life, His death or His resurrection. This is what the New Testament tries to tell us. Sometimes it's pretty involved language, such as this: "If a law had been given which had power to bestow life, then indeed righteousness would have come from keeping the law. But Scripture has declared the whole world to be prisoners in subjection to sin, so that faith in Jesus Christ may be the ground on which the promised blessing is given, and given, to those who have such faith" (Gal. 3:21,22, NEB).

What the Apostle Paul was saying about Jesus Christ was simply this, that we couldn't make it by ourselves, by living up to the law, by being righteous and good. Only through faith in Christ can we be born anew: "If righteousness comes by law, then Christ died for nothing" (Gal. 2:21, NEB).

God brings about a spiritual renewal in your life. You can be willing, but you cannot force it by yourself. All I can tell you is to come to Him, to believe in His power, to give yourself unreservedly to Him. "The man who comes to me I will never turn away," said Jesus (John 6:37, NEB). And that means you, even you and I, can approach Him in confidence and faith.

So, don't get the idea that all I'm saying as a Christian is to force yourself and try harder. That's not good news. That's not liberating. "I have strength for anything through him who gives me power," wrote Paul (Phil. 4:13, NEB). *I have strength* is an affirmation of faith. *For anything,* even to quit a bad habit. And that includes alcoholism. How? *Through him who gives me power.* Through Jesus Christ. He gives me power. I can do all things not in my own power, but in His.

Does this prayer mean anything to you: "O Lord, give me grace to do what I can, that You may give me power to do what You will."

One other point strikes me about those who have made it over the hump. They are completly honest. Steps four and five of A.A. are: "We made a searching and fearless moral inventory of ourselves. We admitted to God, to ourselves, and to one other human being the exact nature of our wrongs." Do you understand now why I asked you all those searching questions earlier?

Sure it's going to be hard to sit down with your family and admit you've been a heel. It's going to be tough to tell your boss that you've suddenly awoken to the fact that you've been unreliable at times and didn't really deserve some of the kindness that's been extended to you. But the most difficult task will be to face up to yourself! You've been a phony! Underneath all that fake stimulation you were scared to death and bitter and perhaps bored with life. That's the truth. You can't hide it any longer. It's hard to face reality, but it's better than living in a fog.

Just think—what a relief. What a relief to have it over with. What a relief to breathe some fresh air. What a relief to start over. What a relief to cut the chain with the past. . . .

One final note, Bob. You will have to live with the fact that you're never cured. It takes only one drink (for you) to step back on the treadmill to disaster. That's a humiliating admission to have to make, but on the other hand it's being honest. It takes courage to make that admission, a courage which many people lack. That's why they never become free from their enslaving habits. It's not a sign of weakness to refuse a drink. It's actually a sign of inner strength.

Years ago Moses gave his people Israel a final warning before he died: "I have set before you life and death, blessing and cursing. Therefore choose life that both you and your seed may live" (Deut. 30:19). I say to you in those ancient words of Moses, choose life that you and yours may live.

I know that this letter has been hard-hitting and tough to take. But I mean it, Bob. You'll have to make the choice. You can't fake it any longer. Choose life with a capital "L." "I have come that men may have life, and may have it in all its fullness," said Jesus (John 10:10, NEB). And He will never reject you, if you come in faith.

In the name of Him who can give us grace to do what we can and power to do what He wills,

Yours,

9

Letter to
a Man in Jail

Dear Bert,

I'm glad you did write. When you were transferred to another city, you knew that it would not be easy for me to visit you in prison, although should you ever want me to come I'd be glad to make the trip. In the meantime the best we can do is correspond.

The one note that you play over and over in your letter is that note of bitterness—a bitterness you feel not only against society but everybody. I know how disappointed you were to lose the battle in the courtroom. You expected to walk out a free man. How often you mentioned that to me before your trial came up. But now you're becoming increasingly bitter. You believe people are out to get you, and you even suspect that your lawyer didn't believe in you. He was only after the money.

"I expect the worst from people, and usually I'm not disappointed," you wrote. And in *your* present circumstances, Bert, I can somewhat understand your hostility. But I can't sympathize. You will need to fight your hatred, and perhaps I can give you some tools with which to do it.

As to your innocence or guilt, let me repeat what we've discussed before. It's not mine to judge you. I'm neither judge nor jury. I'm an interested and concerned friend, who hopes to introduce you to the best Friend you could ever have. So, let's keep the record straight. It doesn't really matter what I think, and you must not attempt to read condemnation into my words. You know me better than that. I'm not your judge.

Back to the bitterness. What is the cause for it? Why do you feel bitter? Why are you so hostile? What are the reasons for this reaction? I don't mean to search out the more immediate causes—your arrest, your trial, the unfortunate sentence—but to probe into underlying reasons, such as your upbringing, your home environment, your experiences in life. All these contribute to the person which you have turned into. And this means that there are many factors which contribute to the bitterness you presently feel.

I remember a man who told me about an experience which he had when he was a young boy. It remains as the most vivid memory of his childhood. His father told him to stand up on a six-foot high wall. The boy was four or five at the time, and his father told him to jump. He held out his arms to his son, but as the boy jumped his father pulled back and allowed his son to fall to the ground, hard. Then he told his befuddled child: "This is how the world will treat you, son. You'd better learn it early."

Can you see why that particular man may have problems similar to yours? He won't trust anyone. He is very suspicious, and that's not really so very strange. But if once he understood the cause for his suspicions, he might be able to cyphen off some of the blame to his father rather than carrying all that hostility himself.

You have probably seen your share of disappointments in your childhood, nor were you spared one of the bitter shocks when you discovered that your wife had been unfaithful. I remember that it made a deep impression on you, because we talked about it many times. You never did get over it. You had an unfortunate marriage. You were both so young.

But, Bert, I know some men who have stepped up from similar disasters. One man was willing to become a father to an illegitimate son born in his own home. His wife confessed her unfaithfulness. Every time he sees that boy which is not actually his own, he is reminded of that betrayal, and a pain pierces his inner self. But he does not allow himself to dwell on that. He keeps shoving it out of his mind and relates to all his children as a father should.

That may seem incredible to you, I know. You may think he is just plain stupid. But, on the other hand, by stepping up from such deep emotional hurt, such a man has changed his wife through compassion and active forgiveness, and has changed himself into a merciful person. Mercy is always superior to judgment. As the Bible says, "mercy triumphs over judgment" (James 2:13, NEB).

That's what I'm really after in your life—change. Of course it's true that people are not to be trusted foolishly. You are pretty close to the gospel when you declare your skepticism regarding man as such. Man is a fallen creature. And from all we can see on this planet, there isn't anything he won't stoop to. All manner of atrocities, every form of crime, every known corruption or deviation he has been guilty of. Nothing is outside of his sphere of defection in body, mind or spirit.

But you can't revenge yourself on the whole human race! You are burning up with this desire for revenge. You are consumed, as if by a fire, to even the score. The trouble with this fire is that it may consume *you*.

You will recall the biblical saying: "Vengeance is mine; I will repay, saith the Lord" (Rom. 12:19). When we take justice into our own hands, we become small. Bitterness is the result of hateful vengeance on our part. Somehow or other, sooner or later justice will be wrought. This is what it means to believe in a just, holy and sovereign God. How can God's kingdom come unless there is first punishment of all evil? How can God's will be done, unless all that is contrary to that will is removed? How can truth triumph unless falsehood is swept away? How can the new heaven and earth come into being, unless the old is destroyed?

The question I want to raise about hatred and hostility is simply this: What is this doing to *you*? How can you live with your conscience? Are you willing to throw away everything? What about eternity? You will have to live with yourself forever. You may not believe that yet. You may still hold, as you have in the past, that the end is the end and when you're dead, you're dead. O.K. That's your privilege, of course. But what if you're mistaken?

You are somewhat of a gambler. What if you are wrong about eternity? There's always that chance, and the odds are even—fifty-fifty. Suppose there is a heaven and hell. Is it worth it to take a blind risk and lose the whole show? Why be a loser? Can't you stick with the winners? No matter what society's verdict, you have your eternal soul to consider, your conscience, your self. Therefore, what you turn yourself into and what you become as a person is of prime importance!

You wrote: "No one has ever taken time to make a better human being out of me." Perhaps that is an overstatement. No one? No one at all? At any rate, you have a responsibility to yourself. It's still your choice as long as you are in this world to become a better human being or a worse one. If you fail here, you may lose the ballgame.

But if you can accept it, there is one who will make a better human being out of you, and who will take the time to do it. He has come into this world for the salvation of all men. Not just for the Christians. Jesus spent His time and gave His life to demonstrate God's compassion for those who were out of it, for the lost, the so-called sinners, the people who never felt welcome at church. He became their friend. And then He died for them. One reason why the establishment put Him to death is simply due to the fact that He wouldn't give up His friendships with the poor, the disinherited, the rejected and the guilty. "It is not his will for any to be lost, but for all to come to repentance" (II Pet. 3:9, NEB). Yes, even you, Bert. Even you.

I realize that you keep maintaining your innocence. As I've told you before, I'm not your judge. Whether you are guilty or innocent only you know. Perhaps I can only sum it up in one of three ways. Either you are guilty; or you are guilty but maintain your innocence; or you are innocent. Let me take these in order.

If you are guilty you can be forgiven. I would rather have you admit that guilt than hide behind the false front of innocence. When you are indeed guilty of something, it's better to spill it all out and get rid of it. "For sin pays a wage, and the wage is death" (Rom. 6:23, NEB).

You may wonder whether it is possible for you to be forgiven. You don't even expect it. You are not the first to think that way. But if the Bible speaks of Moses' forgiveness after his murder of an Egyptian, and David's forgiveness though he took another man's wife, who are you not to believe in the mercy of the Lord? "The Lord is merciful and gracious, slow to anger, and plenteous in mercy. . . As the heaven is high above the earth, so great is his mercy toward them that fear him. As far as the east is from the west, so far hath he removed our transgressions from us" (Ps. 103:8–12).

You can discover for yourself how often Jesus demonstrated the mercy of God by His actions. He freely forgave people like the woman who was caught in adultery, the tax gatherer who had swindled a whole town, or the thief who died for his crimes on a cross next to Him. That condemned man was promised in his midnight hour that he would be in paradise with Christ. He could hardly believe it himself, but Jesus said

72

so and Jesus obviously meant it. It later dawned on that thief that he was forgiven. Even he.

Your other alternative is not so pleasant. If you maintain that you are innocent when in reality you are guilty, you create a huge problem. I don't mean to imply that I consider you guilty. But if you are afraid to admit your breaking of the law because it may lessen your chances in court, you create a spiritual problem for yourself, a problem of playing charades with God. And that can't be done. Not with God.

The man who insists that there is nothing to be forgiven for will never be forgiven. He is like those self-righteous prigs whom Jesus himself was unable to reach. They thought that there was nothing wrong with them. And yet some of them pressed for his trial and called for his crucifixion.

Finally you may indeed be innocent. You have been condemned in spite of that innocence. All you can do legally is to work for a new trial, make appeals, and seek out whatever legal aid you can afford.

But here also something is taking place in your life which has spiritual implications. You may rebel because of the wretched pill you have been forced to swallow, or you can mellow under this oppression into the kind of person you have always dreamed of becoming. You are held in prison wrongfully. You are a little like that man who was found guilty of murdering his wife, but thirteen years later was acquitted and released.

You would not be the first man condemned wrongfully. Have you really considered the fate of Jesus, who was condemned to the cross even though He was completely innocent? Nor are you the first to be imprisoned while guiltless. Did you know that many of our New Testament letters were written from prisons? The apostles were often in jail, and Paul seemed to visit one jail after another not necessarily because of his own choosing. From his cells he wrote several letters which are still preserved in the Scriptures.

Among these letters which are sent to Timothy, Titus, Philemon and the Colossians, Philippians is particularly noteworthy because it leaves the impression of an inner peace, even exhilaration from the apostle. His theme could be summed up in his words: "Rejoice in the Lord alway: and again I say, Rejoice" (Phil. 4:4). Here is not a bitter man in that Roman prison who spews out his hatred, but one who has learned to endure pain and persecution through faith in Christ.

Consider this: "I have learned, in whatsoever state I am, therewith to be content" (Phil. 4:11). That was not written from an half acre estate with a swimming pool in the backyard, but from a three by eight cell. And you cannot help but admire a man who was beaten with thirty-nine stripes laid across his back on five occasions, who faced death, lived through famine, poverty and other threats on his life, who three times was struck with rods and even once stoned and left for dead.

"I have learned contentment? In whatever place or situation?" Unbelievable! And yet, there it is. How can this be? You'll have to take Paul's word for it. It can only happen through Jesus Christ. He transforms life. He really does. That is the evidence which radiates from those letters, the evidence of a joyful assurance which comes through knowing Christ as Savior and Lord.

I would wish this for you, Bert. It will remake your life and ultimately your eternal destiny. While you are in prison may I suggest that you read these prison epistles of Paul? And if they should lead you to Jesus, don't be afraid to come to Him who assures us that He is actually with us to the end of the world.

Prayerfully yours,

10

*Letter to
a Neurotic*

Dear Sue,

When you wrote that you thought you were headed for a
nervous breakdown, let me be honest enough to say that I
didn't receive the news with consternation. I realize that you
have been overanxious for some time, and you have your
moods of depression. But as to a nervous breakdown, I think
you can *avoid* it.

Does that sound strange? Usually people who believe that
their nerves are shot to pieces picture themselves on a slide
which must inevitably lead to a breakdown. But it isn't true. I
once heard a famous psychiatrist say that people engineer their
own breakdowns. It doesn't happen to them. They cause it to
happen! It's a little like talking yourself into a sickness. You
think you are sick, or you are going to get sick, and then you
come down with it.

So, if that psychiatrist said that we actually create our own
breakdowns, then it would seem possible for us to avoid them
as well. Right? Now, *why* do we talk ourselves into a

breakdown? That's not so difficult to figure out. We want a change. We want out. We can't stand a particular situation in which we find ourselves, and this is one way to gain relief. Of course you don't tell this to yourself consciously, but your subconscious is at work all the time. It feeds you dissatisfaction, frustration, and all that unhappiness about your circumstances. The only way to escape may be to have yourself a nervous breakdown. Why not? But, of course, it's not a way out.

Look at it this way. When you can't get to sleep, which is a problem to about fifty percent of Americans, what do you do? No problem. You're supposed to swallow snoozy-woozys and you'll get to sleep. But you haven't solved the problem! In fact now that you're beginning to rely on sleeping pills, you've added another.

Tranquilizers, which surely do some good or else they wouldn't be prescribed by so many capable physicians, are supposed to form a barrier between your emotions and your actual living. They calm the inner self. But do they? Only momentarily. Until you take your next pill. Besides the problems remain, because they have only been treated on the surface. So, instead of showing us how to deal intelligently with our tensions and anxieties, we just fill more prescriptions at the drug store.

A nervous breakdown is only a prolonged tranquilizer. When it's over you must still face life—*your* life. Furthermore, Sue, what nerves break down? If it's something physical following an operation, that's different of course. But I'm thinking of your composite anxieties and tensions. Let's take a look at some factors that may be contributing to your neurosis.

Would it be possible that one of those factors is *jealousy*? I'm thinking of an incident in the Bible where Jesus came to the house of Martha and Mary for dinner. Martha went out to the kitchen to slave over her pots and pans. And I mean she slaved. She wanted to entertain her honored guest in style, and she went to a lot of trouble. In the meantime her sister, Mary, was in the living room listening to Jesus. She hardly gave a thought to all the work that needed to be done. But Martha wanted her sister to help with the work, and she was jealous of Mary as she sat at Jesus' feet. A woman's place is in the kitchen!

Now I suppose you won't blame Martha too much, but even if you want to stick up for her, can you sense the nervous tension building up in her? Why? Jealousy.

Are you jealous, Sue? Of whom? Why? Are you jealous of other women who do not have to work as hard as you? Jealous of those who have been able to continue their careers as you once began until you were forced to keep house? Jealous of your friends who married more money, and can afford help while they flit about socially? And is it possible that these jealous thoughts also turn toward your husband who is free to travel about the country as he pleases, while you're tied to the house and the children? Is this why you are depressed, why you may want a change, and why you're thinking of a nervous breakdown?

Closely akin to this jealousy is another contributing factor—*self-pity*. Here is Martha again in her kitchen, while Mary sits at Jesus' feet. She is cooking over a hot stove, preparing this sumptuous dinner, and she feels sorry for herself. Why should she do all the work? Finally she comes flying out the kitchen door and turns on Jesus: "Lord, don't you *mind* that my sister has left me to do everything all by myself? Tell her to get up and help me!" (Luke 10:40, Phillips).

When you begin to dwell on yourself, you increase your dilemma. Did you know that those who think of others seldom have breakdowns? They haven't the time to. They are too concerned about other people's troubles to worry about their own. But self-pity nurses anxiety. "I can't help feeling sorry for myself," you say. Are you sure? Who else can help it?

I know it's harder for some people than for others, Sue. We all have our own battles to fight, but it's too easy to make

77

excuses for ourselves. Nor can you blame the fact that you were born under some sign, some star, at some time of the month over which you had no control—as a number of people seem to make their alibis. Can you imagine this sort of defeatism rising from the New Testament? No! It is not reasonable to defeat ourselves by such rationalizations. The fickle finger of fate is not pointed at you.

There is one other factor which will make you head for a nervous breakdown, and that is *conflict*. Every person who is a bundle of nerves is also a person who can't resolve those conflicts, whatever they may be. There is only one answer; resolve those conflicts. Obvious? Sure. Find your way through whatever situation keeps you spinning your wheels, or else, you discover that you are taking out your conflicts on your children, your husband and your relatives.

If you have been trying to get at some unpleasant task for weeks, get at it. Do it. If you have been meaning to write a certain letter, write it, and have it over with. If you must ask forgiveness from someone, pick up the phone and stop brooding about it. Resolve your conflicts. Whatever can be changed in your life, approach it constructively.

All this applies to another contributor to our hang ups, perhaps the most potent of all—*guilt*. The only way to resolve the corrosive effect that guilt has upon the human spirit, is to give it to Him who has born it for you. There is a good reason why the Bible tells us: "Surely he hath borne our griefs, and carried our sorrows . . . he was wounded for our transgressions, he was bruised for our iniquities . . . we have turned every one to his own way; and the Lord hath laid on him the iniquity of us all" (Isa. 53:4-6). The blackest sin can be purged. God offers us pardon. Christ has carried our sins upon the cross. He died in our place so that we can be free. The conflict of guilt can be resolved.

Of course if you break a leg it takes a while to heal. A sick mind, one that has been flashing nervous breakdown for some time, will not be cured in a moment. But if forgiveness for sin can become a reality, if conflicts can be resolved, if jealousy and self-pity and all other contributing causes can be faced, healing will take place. Not by means of more pills, but by cutting out the root of your nervous tensions. That is what the good news of Christ should and will accomplish.

But there is even more! Consider this tremendous statement from the Psalms as an alternative to our neurotic tendencies: "Cast thy burden upon the Lord, and he shall sustain thee" (Ps. 55:22). Or this similar verse from the New Testament: "Casting all your care upon him; for he careth for you" (I Pet. 5:7). Throw all your weight upon God, your burden, your lot, your tensions, everything.

Why can you place it all on Him? Because He cares for you. How do you know this? Because of what Jesus has told us about the Father, because it is the Word of God! That is the reason why a Christian dares to live in confidence and faith.

Do you get the picture, Sue? As you let Him support you, He will keep you from falling apart. The Bible says that the everlasting arms of God are underneath. Therefore when your burdens are on the Lord, they are no longer yours. Then what is there to be nervous about?

You see, most of us who believe in God, do not really believe _God_. We believe that Jesus is the Savior of the world, but we don't believe _Jesus_. We believe what the Bible says about faith, but we do not have _faith_. If we did, we would in simple child-like trust experience freedom from anxiety and nervous tension.

Let me put it this way. You won't get me into a spaceship to the moon. Perhaps in years to come we'll take excursions to other planets much as we now fly to Hawaii. But not yet, thank you. I mean, I believe in the scientists and what they are doing, but for now the astronauts will have to do my space traveling for me. I believe in them, but not enough to board a spaceship to the moon tomorrow.

Do we believe in God enough to take that spiritual ride of faith? Or must we continue to bear our burdens alone? When you fly in a plane do you set your luggage on your lap, or check it into the luggage department? Why then carry your own bundles of nervous anxiety?

Remember what Jesus said about the birds of the air and the lilies of the field? They are always looked after by the heavenly Father, who attends His garden and feeds His animals. Now, you are *His child.* Is God not much more interested in His children than in the birds and flowers, even as you are far more concerned about your children than your pets or your garden? So, if God takes care of His creation and animals, will He not much more take care of you, oh you of little faith?

I have not yet commented on one statement in your letter. You added, wistfully I think, "but you don't really know my situation." True, but God does. Do you mean to say that you have something to be nervous about? Is there something that God cannot handle? You don't believe that, do you? That would be a form of pride, because you believe your problem is too big for God. Your anxieties have to be borne by you alone, you must have your nervous breakdown, because God cannot help you at all? You can see how ridiculous this sounds, when all the while He promises you: I will keep you "in perfect peace, whose mind is stayed" on Me (Isa. 26:3).

And there's the key—if your mind is stayed on Him rather than on your many problems.

When our children were six-months-old or so, I could pick them up, swing them around, hold them over my head, or throw them up in the air. They smiled and chuckled and made happy sounds. They enjoyed the danger of being tossed about because they trusted their father. They faced danger with security.

Life holds its dangers for us all. But you can face even your situation with security, since you have a heavenly Father who cares for you.

I have the confidence that you will pull out of this nose-dive, Sue. You don't *have* to have a nervous breakdown, if you will only, fully lean on those everlasting arms.

Prayerfully yours,

11

*Letter to
a Man Who
Is Bored*

Dear Larry,

So you're bored. I suppose most people face boredom not only
once but several times during their lives. It may even increase
in intensity as they get older. How did you put it? You're
bored to death? That's an interesting expression, Larry, *bored
to death*. And yet we don't die. We manage to keep on going
and diverting ourselves from such things as boredom.

Have you ever asked yourself why we have made the
cocktail hour a national institution? Or why do we have to stop
off for a couple of beers before going home? I'm not condemning the practice just now, just raising the question. Is the pace
too hectic? Are we so tense and jittery? Are we afraid of life so
that we cannot face an evening at home, cold sober? It's all a
dreadful escape; but not very different from the people who
stay up every night looking at T.V.—just sitting there before
the box to be entertained.

Funny, isn't it? We live in the one nation of the world which
has more entertainment than any people before us have ever

had; around the clock if you want it. The music must always play and the lights must never go out, because we are bored! Why? What makes us empty? That is your question, Larry, and I'm getting to it.

I suppose that some people are simply bored with the monotony of life. Life is the same, day after day. Your wife has her daily routine, the same house to clean, the same beds to make, the same meals to prepare, the same dishes to wash, the same programs to listen to. Nothing very glamorous. And your schedule is pretty pat, too. You drive the same freeway, plow through the same traffic jams, enter the same office, see the same people, solve the same problems, and then inch your way back home. What for? And yet your job offers some diversion. What of the laborer who has the same mechanical task to perform, hour after hour?

Back in 1882, Harper's magazine printed an article on the problems of living in New York: "His life is a dull, wearisome round, his most serious thought how he shall get on, and while still thinking of it the cord snaps, and the end comes." As Ernest Hemingway wrote in the Snows of Kilimanjaro: "It's a bore," he said out loud. "Anything you do too bloody long."

There are other causes for boredom. For example, are you sometimes bored for no reason at all? You can't really put your finger on it, but you don't want to be around people, and then you do, and when you do, you don't. You pass through dull periods not knowing exactly what you want, while underneath is an aching emptiness.

One of the biographers of Ulysses S. Grant wrote of the Union General before Lincoln gave him full command, that a "fondness of drink seemed to stay with him, although it is notable that he never indulged it when the chips were down. His benders always took place in dull periods, when nothing much was going on." Did you catch that? *When nothing much was going on.* In those interminable dull periods Grant had to escape. Somehow.

When Lew Hoad was twenty and at the threshold of a fabulous career in tennis, he played a routine match. Hoad won the first set but played so poorly that he lost the second and third, while his own fans in Australia booed him. He rallied to win the match but explained later: "I am never bad tempered, but I just didn't want to play tennis during those sets. I got to the stage where I was fed up with everything." Why? No reason. Just bored.

Now I'd like to add to all this that the main reason why we are bored is because we don't have a purpose for living. We may not have discovered one, or else we have lost that purpose, or we fail to see any meaning to our existence. Whatever it may be, we hardly concern ourselves with life's purpose. Whoever takes time to think about a goal? How often do we ask ourselves what it's all about, where we are going, or why we are here? You can't hear all those questions while the traffic buzzes around you, or the music comes down from cloud nine.

I read about a group of savages who are afraid of certain bird sounds. They believe them to be a bad omen. They won't begin to build a village unless the birds are quiet. And if the birds should sing while they are at work, they play their music so loud, and beat those drums so hard, that they cannot hear the birds any more. So, how can we hear anything about the purposes of eternity while all this din rings in our ears?

Now maybe you will understand why you're bored, Larry. You're bored because you really don't know why you are alive. And yet all the while you keep on feeding yourself with all sorts of entertainment, work, business, activity, all the stuff of which life is made. But the trouble is on the inside. Your boredom isn't in these things; it arises from within you. Therefore it's obvious that you can't eliminate boredom by filling yourself up with more movies, more drinks, more sex, more ice cream.

There's a devastating insight in a verse in Proverbs: "Hast

thou found honey? eat so much as is sufficient for thee, lest thou be filled therewith, and vomit it" (Prov. 25:16). You see? Even too much honey is no good. Too much honey and no goal.

If that's clear, Larry, then here comes the real question. What can you do about boredom? That's what you asked me, after all, and I want to move from analysis to solutions.

We talked about life's monotony. Your wife and her household chores, and your daily trips to the office. How do you endure the monotony and boredom of routine?

We have a cat, Larry. I've sat in the backyard, writing and watching her, wondering what she does all day while we rush around. She has no schedules to keep, no business appointments, no telephone to answer, nothing to shop for, no clothes to wash or wear or mend, no meals to cook or dishes to clean, and no television to watch. What in the world does she do all day?

She sleeps and eats and washes herself, comes to be petted and wants to be played with. But when she's not doing any of those things, she is constantly investigating. As if around every plant, behind every bush there lies a new adventure. She is fascinated by a little blowing leaf. She studies the earth for long periods at a time to watch a tiny insect at work. Even a blade of grass is a mystery as it moves in the breeze. She lolls in the sun and turns herself over in the dirt. She chases a bird or a butterfly, but she never seems bored. Never bored!

Have we lost that sense of wonder, that awe for simple things like the warmth of the sun, the beauty of a flower, the majesty of the ocean, the blowing of the wind, the breath of life in the presence of God? Have we lost the sense of mystery? Can we no longer sing "Twinkle, twinkle, little star, how I wonder what you are" because we know of what substance the stars are made? Science has given us too many facts.

But Jesus comes to tell us that we should be as little children and look with eyes of faith. And it will require such child-like eyes of faith to believe that God can transform my work, that God can break into my life, yes, even into my ordinary *blah* life.

As for those inexplainable attacks of boredom, those dull periods that defeated Grant more than any battle he ever fought and slew Hoad on the tennis court. Of course you could get away from it all, have a change in the routine, take a trip. Sure that may help, but it's only a temporary change in the scenery and not in the play itself.

Let me suggest that these dull periods unobtrusively slip into our lives because we're homesick. Remember when you were in the service? Everybody was constantly longing to get back home. Except for sex it was the number one topic of conversation. They dreamed of that patch of ground in Kansas, the familiar homestead in Indiana, or the family they left behind in California. But this earth homesickness is only an illustration of something bigger. Nietzsche cries out almost wildly: "Where is my home?"

The Bible answers Nietzsche when it pictures us as homeless wanderers, pilgrims and strangers in the earth, who look for a city which has foundations, "whose builder and maker is God" (Heb. 11:10). We long for our true home, and that is with God.

Or take Jesus' parable of the son who wanders into the far country away from his father's home. Jesus tells us that he can come home again. And so can we, because there is a Father who loves us, and there is a home to which we may return. Our Father waits for us with open arms, and we will be welcome in spite of our rebellion, rejection and going astray. The door is open, for Jesus has opened the door Himself.

Don't you see, Larry, how this one truth will give us meaning and direction? This one fact makes us aware of the purpose for living? No longer do I have to fill myself with all those empty husks of the world. There is something else I can do. I can live with a sense of God, in the presence of God, with the assurance that this God cares about me. He is not some blind Force, some majestic Power, some disinterested Deity, but a Father who loves and suffers.

But don't get the idea that this purpose and meaning relates only to some distant heaven. Not at all. When Jesus came, He used this phrase over and over again: "The kingdom of God is at hand" (Mark 1:15). Do you understand this? It's not up there in the clouds, not far ahead somewhere in the future, it is *at hand, now,* actually present. And this realization can chase away our boredom. It really can.

Let me offer one final thought. What happens when you laugh at something? Suppose a comedian is really funny and he breaks you up. You sit there laughing your head off, getting a bang out of every joke. What's happening? You are completely involved through this funny guy, and you forget everything else for a few seconds. You chase away all your problems, at least for the moment, even your boredom.

There is a divine laughter, a far more real laughter which not only chases away boredom for the moment, but through which you can laugh away all the devils of boredom, frustration and discouragement. Every time you laugh you involve your whole self, just as you do when you laugh at the stupid antics of some clown. Only when you are indifferent to his nonsense will you sit there with a long face, oblivious to the whole bit.

What am I talking about? Jesus says: "When a woman gives birth to a child, she certainly knows pain when her time comes. Yet as soon as she has given birth to the child, she no longer remembers her agony for joy that a man has been born into the world. Now you are going through pain, but I shall see you again and your hearts will thrill with joy" (John 16: 21-23, Phillips). What has happened? She has forgotten her sorrow and pain of childbirth and joy takes over. She can actually laugh!

Through this illustration Jesus explained to His disciples

that they would laugh again. So, if you can rejoice in the victory of Christ, in His triumph over sin and death and the good news of the home that is prepared for us, you will bring your whole self into this victory. It takes total involvement of the total self!

Only if you sit there like a dodo and don't care about this triumph, only if you reject the eternal purpose that is found in Him who is the way, the truth and the life, only then will you continue on a meaningless excursion to further boredom. But the more you accept the good news of Christ, the more you begin to laugh *on the inside*. The more you allow Christ into your life, the more inner joy replaces the need for outer stimulation. For this is the victory that overcomes the world, even our faith. (You will find this spelled out in I John 5:4,5).

I'm not going to state flatly that you will never again have attacks of boredom. Not at all. But at least you will know why you have these attacks and how to meet them. Through Jesus Christ we pilgrims discover the purpose of life, we who are lost find the way, and we who are sad are granted divine laughter.

If you come right down to it, Larry, the answer to most of our dilemmas (perhaps all of them) is found in the application of the good news of Jesus Christ. May you know the victory and joy that can lift the haze of boredom.

Purposefully yours,

Letters to Christians with Problems

"In the fear of the Lord is strong confidence: and his children shall have a place of refuge."

Prov. 14:26

12

Letter to a Christian with an Inferiority Complex

Dear Ann,

Do you mind if I'm blunt? It seems to me that most of your problems originate from an inferiority complex. I've never come right out and said so before, but I think that we ought to examine the root of the matter.

I suppose that most people have been beset by feelings of inferiority. A person must be superhuman or else non-responsive, if he has not realized some inferior feelings at one time or another. Of course that's a long road toward what is commonly called an inferiority *complex*, but what I'm pointing out is that we are touching on a very human problem.

Let me begin by exploring some of the causes that contribute to an inferiority complex, so that we can then cope with it in a mature fashion. It's pretty obvious that an inferiority complex has one of its roots in childhood. Psychology has explored the enormity of those influences during the formative years, when we grow from six to one hundred pounds in a big hurry. After all, a child *is* inferior to adults in height, weight, stature, strength and mental ability.

Such normal feelings of inferiority cannot be avoided. But now consider the indulgent mother who pampers her children and won't let them grow up. If your parents were overprotective and did not allow you to wash or clothe yourself when you were old enough, this would have made you feel incapable of accomplishing these ordinary tasks. When everything is done for you such as the solving of problems with toys and later homework, then your initiative is stunted.

Or, did your parents favor another child over you? You were number two, weren't you, Ann? Quite often when the first baby arrives, he receives all the attention and the second child faces a different situation at an early age. On top of this, your parents had a girl first and probably hoped for a boy. Then you came. Maybe they showed their disappointment (Did they express it in times of anger?) so that you knew you were not the favored child. And soon it was: "Ginny is bringing home all A's and B's on her report card. Why do you have only C's?" And you began to wonder what was wrong with you?

Well, it won't be necessary to go into all the other incidents which made you feel inferior to your sister, and then to your younger brother who was your father's pride and joy. You will surely recall many of these incidents, since they have been tucked away in your memory. They hurt so much; and perhaps they still do.

But why did I bring up these painful childhood experiences at all? I have a reason, Ann. When you understand why you have these feelings of inferiority, you can begin to get rid of some of them. If your parents pampered and favored another child, or belittled you, this could have had a profound effect on you. You can in perfect conscience *blame them* for that.

Doesn't this run counter to honoring your parents? No. You still love and honor them, but you remember that they are mortal too; and these are facts. You see your upbringing for what it is. You don't tell yourself lies. You don't continue a fantasy, which your subconscious warns you isn't true. That's why you must see it clearly. You are not totally to blame for your inferiority feelings. Not for everything. Others played a part in shaping you into the person you are today—a Christian with an inferiority complex.

My point is that *all* the blame does not rest on your shoulders, and you will have to accept that plain fact.

You can also take an even more positive step. You can grow up. You are no longer a child; you are an adult now. You can mature beyond these childhood influences. They do not have to hamper you for the rest of your life. Why should this remain a burden? "When I was a child, my speech, feelings, and thinking were all those of a child; now that I am a man, I have no more use for childish ways" (I Cor. 13:11, ABS).

That means, of course, that when we are changed from this world to the next, we move in transition from childhood (which is this world) to adulthood (which is heaven). But isn't it literally true as well? We are no longer children when we grow up. Our attitudes change, our outlook changes, our thinking matures. So, grow up. Grow up all the way! You are no longer a child. You can become a mature adult.

A second cause for an inferiority complex lies in our thinking. I remember one man who was concerned about what he called "stinking thinking." He had a lot of changing to do and he kept on with it, although it was painful and difficult for him. We all have some stinking thinking to change. As a man thinks "in his heart, so is he" (Prov. 23:7). You are what you think. When you see yourself as accomplished, desirable, beautiful, courteous, thoughtful or self-assured, you tend to behave in like manner. But dwell on your failures and your faults and you lose much self-confidence.

A very attractive girl attended a party. Soon some admirers gathered around her and the conversation turned to her beauty. Someone complimented her. "Well, thank you," she said, "but look at my hands." At this she thrust out her hands which were red and swollen as a result of a disease. From then on she lost her attractiveness for people. All they could think of was her hands. And why? Because all she could think of was her hands. She had forgotten all her other attributes.

Why then, Ann, should you allow yourself to dwell on those things which make you feel inferior to others? You project your fears to other people and believe them to be critical of you, when in reality they may not be criticizing you at all. Yet you set a vicious circle in motion because of your projections. Then you dislike yourself for being like this, and because you feel inferior you then look down even more on yourself, which in turn makes you feel more inferior. And so on and on, ever downward into your own special little pit.

Again, excuse me if I'm too blunt, but isn't it better to wake up to what we are doing to ourselves? Samuel Shoemaker wrote that "self-hatred is as great a sin as self-love". Do you understand that? Self-hatred is not humility. Self-hatred is destructive. It is contrary to the teaching of Jesus, for He taught that we should love our neighbor *as ourselves.* But how can we love them if we hate ourselves? We will only tolerate others, or put on a show while inwardly we feel very uneasy in their company, since (as before) we consider ourselves so inferior. And for all that we actually despise ourselves the more.

What can you do about this stinking thinking, about this negativism? One answer is to think positively. No question about that. But more important even is the necessity to be realistic about yourself. You are what you are. And that's an important concept to take hold of.

When people praise you, that does not change you into a better person. Criticism may deflate you, but that cannot alter the real you either. Whether you are praised or criticized, you remain what you are. They may pin a medal on your chest, place a ribbon around your neck, fill your arms with flowers and give you the key to the city, but in the end you are what you are, no matter what they may say. Good or bad. Isn't that true? No one can make you feel inferior, unless *you* allow them to.

Therefore, why should you think of yourself destructively? Why do you consider yourself worthless? You will probably answer: "I don't only think I'm inferior, I *am* inferior. That's me. That's the way I am". And you allow yourself to believe this, but do you realize, Ann, that this is far removed from true Christianity?

What does it mean to be a Christian? Doesn't this mean that God looks upon you as His child, and not inferior, since He has accepted you? He does not consider you worse than all the other sinners in the world. Jesus has given His life for all of us. He has died *for you, too.* The love of God is for the world, and that includes everyone who has fallen short of the mark of perfection. God is no respecter of persons. He has no favorites. Some may be big sinners, some middle-sized and some small, but all of us are equally in need of salvation. There is no difference, "that every mouth may be stopped, and all the world may become guilty before God" (Rom. 3:20).

Now this means that if Jesus died for you, as you most certainly believe, then you are accepted by Him. He really loves you. He really forgives you. You are a child of God. And if you are, how can you continue to feel inferior? You are a member of the family of the eternal God. You, along with everyone else who believes in Jesus Christ, belong in that family of faith. You are no longer unworthy. You are not inferior. And you are what you are by the grace of God!

Think of yourself as a child of God. That's what you are. You have already been accepted.

But you also wrote, Ann, that you have failed so terribly

and so often. You cannot see any accomplishments in your life, and certainly no victories. Everything turns out to be a bleak landscape of failure for you.

Well, our failures are real enough. But they need never be final. I *made* a failure does not mean I *am* a failure. There is no such equation. No matter how many times you have failed (and everyone fails innumerable times), you only become a failure when you cannot rise again from your mistakes. But I believe you can prevent yourself from forming a complex about this, and I'm sure you will make every effort to pick yourself up and start walking again.

There was a prophet named Jeremiah who was called of God, but he objected. He felt unworthy of becoming a prophet. "I am a child," he said. "I cannot speak" (Jer. 1:6). God told him not to think like that and offered Jeremiah his presence in his prophetic work. But Jeremiah had a giant inferiority complex which was aggravated by the way he thought of himself as a failure and as a little child, who couldn't do anything right. Everything we've been talking about, rolled up in one person!

But God used even this Jeremiah, as you can tell from his book. "The Lord said unto me, Say not, I am a child: for thou shalt go to all that I shall send thee, and whatsoever I command thee thou shalt speak. Be not afraid of their faces; for I am with thee to deliver thee, saith the Lord" (Jer. 1:7,8).

A sick man lay near a pool in Jerusalem. Jesus wanted to help him, but He did not go up to him and say: "I want to help you. Get up and be healed." Rather He asked the man: "Do you want to get well?" (John 5: 6, ABS). That is the question. Do you really *want* to? Is that your overriding desire? Do you want to become a whole person? Incidentally, that is the biblical understanding of the word "salvation"—to become a whole person. Or do you want to continue with all those inferiority feelings? That is your choice.

God Himself can change you, for He is God. Do you really

96

believe this enough to apply it to yourself? As a Christian you may assent to these doctrines, but how deeply do they penetrate your consciousness? Is Christianity merely a matter of mental assent, or does our faith actually enter the inner dynamics of living?

I'd like you to feel it. Now, please don't misunderstand me on this point. Faith is never feeling. How religious or pious you feel is no indication by which you may gauge whether you are a Christian. To the contrary. Sometimes those who do *not* feel religious are closer to Christ, for the poor in spirit possess the kingdom of God. The pious ones who consider themselves the spiritually elite may through pride fail to experience God's grace.

But what I mean to say about feeling is this: Your faith must not remain a matter of the book. It needs to be translated into living. You know what sometimes happens as you view a play or a performance. You become a part of the action. You may be deeply moved, and something comes through to you. You feel it. There's that word again, and that's what I'm talking about. Does your religious faith get through to your inner self? It ought to. It's the real thing. Salvation is more than any play.

I suppose that the old theologians had this in mind when they expounded the doctrine of the Holy Spirit. They emphasized the fact that the letter itself kills and lacks power. But when the Spirit applies the letter, the word becomes alive and has the power to convert, to challenge, to change. "The written law brings death, but the Spirit gives life" (II Cor. 3:6, ABS).

That is exactly what I hope will happen to you, Ann. You are a Christian. You believe. But you are still plagued by a basic insecurity. Will you allow the Spirit of God to bring the Word of God to you, so that it becomes a part of you?

God does not want you to be His child with an inferiority complex, just as you want your children to grow up secure and happy! You are accepted. You are beloved. He who gave His life for you cares for you so much, that He does not want you to live as an abnormal Christian.

Now I can't do any of this for you, as much as I would like to see you become a mature and whole person. Ann, its up to you to *believe* the good news!

Yours,

13

Letter to
a Christian Who
Has Lost His Faith

Dear Tom,

You evidently think that you have presented me with a curious
dilemma in your letter. You wrote that you have been brought
up since childhood as a Christian and accepted Jesus at an early
age. Now you are losing your faith.

I want to assure you that I have often run into this problem
during my ministry. I can't tell you how many Christians I
have encountered who were raised with Christianity, but who
generally in their twenties (sometimes thirties) had serious
doubts. Some have left the church altogether. Others are
desperately trying to hold on to something they once believed.

So, Tom, you wonder why? You ask whether you can still
believe in Christianity as you once did. You want to accept it,
and yet you find so many contradictions in the world around
you. Your reason produces too many arguments against faith,
and the more you learn, the more you seem to be questioning
simple belief.

My first reaction to all this is that any faith which is not

99

reasonable is not worthy of the name. If we were to believe something illogical, it would not hold true, in spite of the fact that we believed it. Just as if you were asked to believe in a square circle, you couldn't do it. Trying to believe something won't make it so. Since Jesus said that, we dare not leave our minds on the doorstep when we enter the church. We are to worship God with our minds too. Ours is a reasonable faith.

But that is not to imply that faith can be perfectly reasoned out. There is an area into which faith travels beyond logic and reason. Or else faith in God becomes the product of my logic. Then God would not be God in the true sense of the word!

Picture a circle to represent your knowledge, and then project a line through that circle into the space beyond, and you have a picture of faith. The circle is the physical world which you can explore by reason and logic. Faith travels beyond that physical world, beyond our limited field of logic—to God.

"To have faith is to be sure of the things we hope for, to be certain of the things we cannot see," is the biblical definition of faith (Heb. 11:1, ABS). Through faith we believe that God created the heavens and the earth. We can never with total assurance *know* this. No scientist can or will conclusively prove this theory of creation, because none of us were there. Faith affirms God as Creator of all.

By faith we make our way to the city of God. We cannot know that this city exists with absolute certainty, except as we take it as the Word of God. One day faith will see what it has believed (which is, incidentally, a promise of Scripture). But not yet. With all possible reason and logic, and yet by that added dimension of faith "we fix our attention, not on things that are seen, but on things that are unseen. What can be seen lasts only for a time; but what cannot be seen lasts for ever" (II Cor. 4:18, ABS).

But I doubt whether this conversation about faith is getting through to you, since you find so much in life that is contradictory. You see so much suffering. You encounter so many tragedies. You wonder why children are born blind or deformed, why innocent people are killed, why a thousand and one unexplainable mysteries occur, or why injustice, indecency, indulgence and indifference seem to rule the world. (That's a nice bit of stringing words together, Tom.)

I agree with you! There is much in the world that contradicts faith in God. There are even those who have asked why God would allow the crucifixion, if Jesus was His only Son? Didn't He have the power to intervene? The answer is that God possessed the power but did not utilize it. When He sent His Son into the world to die for our sins, He freely allowed the cross for the salvation of mankind. That's why He stayed His hand.

But what would happen if we relied purely on sight? What if we could believe in God and never encountered suffering, tragedy or unexplainable mysteries? Let me illustrate that. Follow me closely now.

There are some who consider the miracles of Jesus proofs of His divinity. The miracles He performed supposedly prove conclusively, that Jesus is the Son of God. Now, if the miracles are indeed proofs, they would be a total appeal to sight. If miracles are conclusive evidence for Jesus, then He would have resorted (and I am going to change my words deliberately) to cheap tricks. This is how a man can call attention to himself, as a magician, to get people to accept him as their king.

But if you know the Scriptures at all, you will immediately recognize that this is the very opposite of what Jesus did. On one occasion they wanted to make him king because of a so-called miracle, but He escaped from their midst. He would have none of it. He almost always told those whom He healed to keep it quiet and not to tell anyone. As for His miracles, they were never a means to call attention to Himself. They were always responses to the needs of people. The blind, the lame, the lepers, the hungry crowd were all in need when Jesus met those needs. They were never tricks to create faith.

You see, if you consider the miracles as good evidence for Christ, there are those who can argue the point. They do not accept the miracles, and therefore do not believe in Christ. When you use the miracles as proofs to lead a person to faith, what if they fail to bring commitment? No—this is the wrong way to proceed.

The person who believes in Christ will also believe the miracles. Faith in Christ precedes the miracles, not the other way around. Or else the miracles would have convinced all who saw them, but the fact is that the Pharisees acknowledged Jesus' miracles, yet still plotted to put Him to death.

Is my point coming through, Tom? Those who argue for miracles will be opposed by those who argue against them. Those who argue for sight, that is sufficient evidence for God in the world, will be opposed by those who see only contradictions to belief in God. And then you end up with two opposing parties and endless arguments between believers and unbelievers.

But faith is something else! It is contained in that arresting phrase about Moses: "He endured, as seeing him who is invisible" (Heb. 11:27). How do you see the invisible? You don't. You only "see" by faith. And that is not living by sight at all, but by the reality of God *in spite of all the contradictory evidence* in the world.

I would like to add, Tom, that as you tunnel through this struggle of faith, the light may be dazzling when you emerge. You can no longer hold to the simple Sunday school pictures which you were shown as a child, nor accept the same childish faith you had when you also believed in Santa Claus. You grew up physically, and now you are growing spiritually. Is that so bad? If you can see it this way, you will look on yourself not with alarm but with confidence of what lies ahead.

In this regard I'd better clarify one remark of Jesus. He told us to have faith as a little child. He did not mean childishness. He spoke of a simple faith which believes in the goodness of God even though we cannot see Him. A young child believes readily. It is a beautiful, almost innocent quality. (Faith sees the invisible!) But childlike trust is not childishness. We should grow out of childishness into the maturity of faith.

Now, faith only grows when it is in a battle with doubt, and as you presently doubt some of your beliefs, the time will come when you will also doubt your doubts. I honestly believe that when you emerge from this phase—and it is a phase—your faith will be stronger, more realistic.

The writer to the Hebrews said in his letter that we must pass on from milk to meat: "Anyone who has to drink milk is still a child, without any experience in the matter of right and wrong. Solid food, on the other hand, is for adults, who have trained and used their tastes to know the difference between good and evil" (Heb. 5:13,14, ABS). The milk corresponds to the fundamentals, and the meat is more solid food. As a child in the faith you were given the milk of repentance, faith, crucifixion, resurrection and eternal judgment. Pretty potent stuff, you say? Sure. But this you have heard. Now, what else is there? What is this meat?

We Christians are far too quickly content to let people accept the fundamentals of the faith, and then call it quits. After all it takes less effort to heat up some milk for a baby, than it does to prepare a good, solid meal built around a tasty meat dish. As long as people are born again we seem satisfied, and we allow them to proceed on their own after their decision. Proceed on what? Where? How?

How many Christians digest the meat of Christian living? How many even give serious thought to practicing the teaching of Christ? When it comes to the hard realities in this dirty world, we dig in and start hitting in all directions. Nobody had better get in our way. Even in the church we find instances of dirty pool and underhanded methods to serve selfish ends. I'd

103

rather not tell you some of those stories, but the question is—if we're supposed to be Christians how is it possible *in the name of God* to behave in un-Christian ways?

What is a Christian? Aren't we supposed to live a different life, in spite of all the opposition that is thrown up against us? So, I would suggest that Christians begin to explore what Jesus has to say to us. *That* is the meat of the word, because that requires a lot of chewing, digesting and living. We have largely by-passed the words of Jesus because they are demanding, and because we enjoy the softer, more comforting doctrines that go down into our minds like mush.

You have lost your faith? Not at all. You just haven't explored its depths— You are wading in the shallow waters of a few Christian beliefs, and now you are tired of splashing around like a kid. You want to swim. You are created to experience the exhiliration of being held up by your faith in the living God, in spite of contradictory evidence in the world. You can swim, Tom. Explore those depths. Discover for yourself what Christ intended you to become. Move beyond the elementals. Take the solid food of His gospel.

One final word. You pride yourself a little, I think, on your namesake, Thomas. Doubting Thomas, as we call him. But do you really know about doubting Thomas? He was a stubborn man who insisted to his friends that he would not believe Jesus had risen from the dead, unless he could see the prints of the nails and the wound in Jesus' side. He refused the evidence of the disciples, who had been his friends for more than three years. That's true enough.

But then Jesus appeared. "Put your finger here—look, here are My hands. Take your hand and put it in My side. You must not doubt, but believe," Jesus said to Thomas (John 20:27, Phillips). Thomas didn't have to touch. Instead he fell down and exclaimed: "My Lord and my God" (John 20:28).

Here was the greatest affirmation of faith that any disciple had yet made. They had called him Lord before, but never

God. And for a Jew named Thomas to affirm that is to admit that the doubter was in reality a man of great faith! "There lives more faith in honest doubt, believe me, than in half the creeds," wrote Tennyson. And Thomas proved it too, by his life. He went preaching the faith (as some traditions hold) as far as India. The Christian church in India traces its origin to Thomas, who was (again according to tradition) shot to death by arrows while in prayer.

I wouldn't mind at all, Tom, if your present struggles lead you to such an affirmation of faith! As soon as you begin to doubt your doubts you will become a man of heroic proportions and Christian living. The world needs more men like this. It has enough doubters, enough half believers and enough traditional Christians who will not leave the bottle to digest the solid food of Jesus' teaching.

In the name of Him who is invisible, but whom we can "see" by faith,

Yours,

14

Letter to
One Who
Can't Pray

Dear Lois,

Thanks so much for your honest letter. "Why should I bother to pray," you ask. You find so little time for prayer, and when you do pray it doesn't accomplish anything for you. You even got rid of that old slogan you had on a plaque from years ago: "Prayer changes things," because things don't change. Nothing seems to be happening, and so you're wondering what prayer is all about after all.

Let you in on a little secret. Many people find prayer difficult. Of course they don't always say so. It sounds heretical. A Christian is supposed to pray, isn't he? A good Christian is supposed to keep up a prayer life. You were taught this when you were young, and it almost seems sacrilegious to question. Don't let that disturb you. Quite a few Christians have given up prayer, and about the only praying they do is that Lord's Prayer in Church, and maybe an occasional quicky before they go to bed.

Now, why? If prayer is simply self-hypnosis—as some

106

non-prayers believe—then it would have disappeared from the earth long before this. If prayer is putting ourselves into a good frame of mind, our scientific friends would have figured that out long ago and therefore dispelled the worth and power of prayer.

The fact is that most people pray almost by instinct. When they get into trouble, they may only say, "O God", but that is a prayer too, don't you think? Prayer rises up from man almost naturally since we are created by God. Animals have instincts too, but man prays when he is in trouble.

This is the most primitive form of prayer, but it is prayer nevertheless. However, if we force ourselves into an unnatural prayer life, if we make ourselves buckle down to certain prescribed duties, our inner self begins to rebel. That may be what is happening to you, Lois. You were given all these prescriptions for prayer and now you are throwing them off. Prayer can be forced. It can become unnatural. It can fail to communicate. And unless prayer is communication with God, it becomes a poor substitute, like artifical flowers that cannot create a natural aroma as real flowers do.

But let's tackle your questions. Prayer doesn't work any more. Nothing happens. You get no answers. You wonder whether you know how to pray. All right.

We live in a culture that may be described as utilitarian. That means that we want everything to work. If something won't work we get rid of it, or let it gather dust in some closet. What good is it? Everything must have a function. And consequently when we discover that prayer is not performing for us as it should, we throw it out. For other people it's faith, or the church, or the Bible, even God. *Results* is the word we underline, and results is what we expect.

Now, it is true that you can expect results from prayer, Bible reading, going to church, or faith in God. But somehow that doesn't sound quite right, does it? What results do you expect from helping someone? What results are to be gained

107

from being kind? Do you love someone for the benefits you receive?

Why should prayer bring results? Isn't prayer supposed to be communication with God? Isn't prayer something that should exist *for itself,* for its own sake, rather than for what it can produce in your life? Any result will be a by-product, but the reality of prayer lies elsewhere. Answers to prayer are incidental; prayer itself, as a means of talking with God, is the goal.

Just suppose that answers to prayer were always yes? What if you received exactly what you asked for, every time? Then would God be God, or would we have transformed Him into some answering machine, a mechanical device that dispensed correct information for us upon request? We program "it" aright, and the answers come flowing out automatically. Then prayer really *works,* of course, and you can use it as a means to obtain what you want. But now we are playing God! God is no longer *God.* Isn't it obvious that you can't always have what you want, or else you would change the heavenly Father into an automated Santa Claus?

So, what is prayer? Is it some utilitarian means of producing answers with about the same consistency that a fruit tree produces fruit? Take good care of your trees: water, feed and prune them, and they'll produce fruit. So also prayer obtains answers if you put in the right ingredients—faith, confession, sincerity and make your request in Jesus' name.

Prayer is far more than that! It includes adoration, confession, thanksgiving and supplication. That's easy to remember, since the first letters of these words spell "acts"—adoration, confession, thanksgiving and supplication. We begin to pray by praising God, acknowledging him as Creator and Sovereign Lord. Our adoration leads us to confession of our sins, for we become aware of our shortcomings. We ask forgiveness. After confession we give thanks for all things that are given us, including the gospel of salvation. Finally comes our supplication, our asking. That's last on the list.

This is also the pattern of the Lord's Prayer, which is a model. We do not immediately launch into petition. We concentrate on the glory of God, pray for the coming of His kingdom and for His will to be done on earth. We hallow His name.

When this has become part of us, we begin to pray about ourselves. But notice *what* we pray for—food, forgiveness and deliverance from temptation. Even our daily bread which we need, is brought to the Father's attention. Not our desires or wants, but our basic needs. We ask forgiveness for our debts as we forgive others and pray for strength in the hour of temptation.

Now I ask you, Lois, is this the pattern of your prayers? Is this how and what most Christians pray about? If we are not afraid to rethink our traditional teaching, prayer can become more potent. We will not be merely brought back to prayer, but we will advance to a better perspective. Prayers will not be childish give-me, give-me requests for heavenly results, but will seek to put us in touch with God. And when everything else has been said, prayer is basically the reality of communication.

Another fact emerges from your questions. Do you just sit back, pray and do nothing? When you work for something, you need not pray for it, and when you pray for it you need not work? No. The alternative to prayer is not work. The alternative to prayer is depression, frustration, anxiety. Jesus put it like this: "Men ought always to pray, and not to faint" (Luke 18:1). This means that prayer is not an alternative to action, but to disillusionment and lack of purpose.

Therefore when you pray you don't simply sit back. Rather you put your prayers into action. If, for example, you pray to be able to overcome a temptation, you do everything possible to keep from yielding when it assails you. You don't passively expect some miraculous deliverance. (Of course we can't overcome temptations all by ourselves. That's why we pray about them).

Similarly if you pray to become loving, you don't wait for love to arrive on angelic wings. You attempt to live kindly, you show compassion, you are merciful, you overcome evil with good, and you learn to live in love. This is what prayer means. Let your prayers be translated into life. Let your prayer be your life and your life be your prayer!

"But if God already knows what we want before we ask Him, why should we pray at all?" That's a legitimate question. It's probably based on these words from the Sermon on the Mount: "God is your Father and He already knows what you need before you ask him" (Matt. 6:8, ABS). But do you understand in what context Jesus said this? He was talking about people who repeated the same requests over and over. "In your prayers do not use a lot of words, as the pagans do, who think that God will hear them because of their long prayers" (Matt. 6: 7). They will *not* be heard for repeating prayers since no one has to impress God with his prayers. No, God knows what you need before you ask. Jesus warned those who would try to impress God with their sincerity and religious zeal.

"What does it mean to say, 'Thy will be done?' Isn't that resigning everything to God? Then why ask for anything?" We find this phrase, 'Thy will be done' in the final prayer of Jesus in the garden of Gethsemane before the cross. He said it not in dumb resignation, nor in fear, but in commitment and faith. Jesus *knew* the Father. In that perfect knowledge He committed himself trustingly to that will.

However, it is important to notice that this phrase comes *after* Jesus actually prayed. In His prayer He asked that the cup would be removed. He did not want to die on the cross! Only following that request, Jesus added: "Not my will, but

110

thine, be done" (Luke 22:42). This means, of course, that the original request was not granted. The cup was not removed. He drank it to the bitter end. But Jesus humbly and willingly accepted His Father's verdict.

We should never pray only that God's will might be done. Say it after you have brought all your petitions to Him. Ask anything at all. But end your requests humbly, as a little child who knows that she may not have asked correctly. Your Father may not consider that answer best for you. *You* think it's best. You think you want it. It's exactly what God should do. But when you pray for His will to be done, you admit that you do not want what *you* want, but what *He* wants for you. And if you really trust Him as your Father, you know that will be the best.

One final thought comes to me. Sometimes we stop praying not because of intellectual difficulties but due to emotional failure. To put it straight—not our doubts but our sins stop us. Have you failed to live up to your expectations? Do you feel guilty? Do you consider yourself unworthy to pray? Then there is only one road back. Confess any known sin. Ask forgiveness.

"He that covereth his sins shall not prosper: but whoso confesseth and forsaketh them shall have mercy" (Prov. 28:13). I am not suggesting that you are covering any sins, but guilt in one form or another may be keeping you from praying.

The king in *Hamlet* who has been responsible for a murder tries to pray: "My words fly up, my thoughts remain below." That's the way it seems when sin is not confessed or forsaken.

But God promises us mercy, His everlasting mercy. (Yes, even for murder.) "The Lord is merciful and gracious, slow to anger, and plenteous in mercy . . . He hath not dealt with us after our sins . . . For as the heaven is high above the earth, so great is his mercy toward them that fear him. As far as the east is from the west, so far hath he removed our transgressions from us" (Ps. 103:8-12). This is the Father to whom we pray.

111

So I suggest, Lois, that you open up communications. You can begin by simply talking to God. He is your Father. And He loves you!

I also suggest that if you want to gain new insight into prayer, that you study the prayers in the Bible. For example, take those in Ephesians one and three. I'm sure that this will change your ideas, for there are few people who pray like this among Christians.

May you not simply be led *back* to praying, but moved *forward* to a more meaningful communication with the One who answers us above all that we ask or think, and gives us not merely answers, but Himself.

Prayerfully yours,

15

Letter to Secular Christians

Dear Walt and Lucy,

So you're fed up with the church. You're not the only ones. I suppose you are aware that the statistics show a drop in church attendance, Sunday school enrollment and giving. In spite of the population explosion, this has become a national trend. Although I must point out that there are some churches in which this is not true, and some denominations that are growing instead of losing.

People have turned away from the church as an institution and only frequent it for a wedding, a baptism or occasionally on Easter. Most of them do not list as many reasons for their departure as you do. You are very explicit in your objections, and I suppose it is best I try to comment on some of these.

You think that generally ministers are dull, not worth listening to, and they don't seem to be excited about their subject. Sometimes they strike you as merely going through the motions, saying what they ought to say. Now, I agree with you, it is hard to find an exciting minister, but they are around. And when you find one, you can be sure that there are people listening to him preach the Word of God. But many ministers feed their flock stones instead of bread, and that in a most unappetizing manner.

If a minister can't be more worked up about the good news than a comedian is about his usually inane routine, if a minister can't be more excited about the gospel of Christ than a football fan is at a game, then why should he be in the pulpit at all? I am not suggesting that ministers put on a show like comedians, or start yelling like football fans. We already have some who put on shows and there are a few who yell because they don't have anything to say. (If they can't expound God's Word, they just pound.) What I am suggesting is that if the good news of Jesus Christ can no more effect a man than make him boring or dull, then the fault lies not with the gospel but with that man.

So I agree heartily with your objection. It is intolerable for a preacher not to preach! Ministers make many excuses for themselves. They are too busy to prepare, they have too many responsibilities in the church, or they say that nobody is interested in preaching anyway. Other forms such as counseling, small groups, teaching, or drama are more valid. Of course those forms are valid, but wherever a man proclaims eternal truth with power, there are live congregations.

Strange, Walt and Lucy, that you haven't been able to find anyone like that, anywhere. They are around, for God has not left Himself without a witness.

You also bring up the question of hypocrisy. And you are right about that too. But hypocrisy covers a wide front. They don't live their Christianity? Check. They claim a lot for themselves but don't act like it? Check again. But who does? Do you? No matter how well you may think of yourselves, no one is perfect. Are we then in any position to criticize? Or are we only condemning ourselves, since we will be judged with the same judgment we measure?

You give an example of church fights. You don't know the half of it. But I suppose you know enough to have a bad taste in your mouth. Christians are not behaving as Christians should, and this is a blot on the church.

But it is necessary to remember that the church is not an institution for saints, but a house for sinners. Isn't this the very place where all must be welcome, and all need to be encouraged to come? Where else can a sinner go? I'm sure you believe this, and yet that allows no excuse for some of the things that happen in churches. We should *not* fight. We should *not* criticize. We should *not* be prejudiced. We should not behave like hypocrites. Most Christians are aware of what they shouldn't do and what they should do. But the power to do it, the power of the Holy Spirit, is lacking in their lives.

To put it straight—it seems to me that we do not allow God to have His way with us, and if we would, we could be living differently. If the Spirit of God controlled us, we would put our faith into practice. We would listen to the teaching of Jesus and behave differently. That certainly is a crying need of the Christian church. No doubt about that.

You also mentioned all those church socials. You are tired of the merry-go-round. If only the church would exert its influence in social matters, rather than just playing around as most Christians do. True again. But if you have taken notice, there are some congregations who are putting their faith into action. The whole church circus is going to come to an end, for God will purify His people. He will use those who are committed to Him, and leave all those others to play their churchianity game. Isn't that precisely what Jesus did when he chose his followers and by-passed the establishment? And he is still calling out disciples in our time.

Yet in spite of the fact that you find the church irrelevant, your letter raises the thoughtful question—what happens now? You still have genuine faith in Christ. You believe in

Him, as your Lord and Savior. You have not denied the faith. As someone has said, you believe in God, but not in His ground crew. So, what happens now? Where do you go from here?

Well, you can proceed without the church as many do. You can simply forget about worship, and you will probably not take time to worship God unless you attend church. You will in all probability read your Bible less. I've discovered that those Christians who are drifting away, open their Bibles very little. And how could the church support any missionaries if everyone deserted? Only as a corporate body is it possible to send missionaries or support social work among the poor and needy.

So the secular Christians drift farther and farther away, unless they find something else. A small group, for instance. There are many such groups around. They're somewhat of an underground movement. The press is not aware of them. And those who belong to the groups don't want any publicity either. They may meet weekly, every two weeks or monthly. Sometimes they study the Bible or a Christian book. Sometimes they meet for discussion. Sometimes you can expect what I might term "Christian therapy." But you will always find the most interesting people. People who have questions. People who are not afraid to discuss their hang-ups. People who do not think that church worship alone suffices.

Such small groups were the backbone of the early church, for those Christians had no sanctuaries for public gatherings. They met in homes, and because of their intimate fellowship, Christianity grew rapidly. Formal worship services have their place, mind you, but through these small groups Christianity flourished. I would strongly urge you to enter such a group, where you can freely share your doubts and your faith, for who knows what this may come to mean to you and where it may lead you?

116

I suppose you have considered the possibility of changing churches. I don't recommend this generally, because once you begins hopping around, you may become like those who travel from one congregation to another. They are never satisfied and they seldom stop criticizing. There is always something amiss. There are no perfect churches. But if you look, you may find a Church where the preacher is not dull, where the congregation is relevantly involved in the world, and where the emphasis is on Christian growth rather than merely enjoying social get togethers. Sounds like the perfect set up, doesn't it?

But, Walt and Lucy, we've forgotten one other fact in answer to your question of *why* we attend church. We go to church to worship God, to fellowship with other Christians, but also to take the opportunity of considering eternal things. We are continually enmeshed in the temporal and the material. We need to regularly rethink directions. What are we here for? Where are we going? What lies beyond death? The church should remind us of our frailty, prepare us for death and make us aware that we will enter eternity.

Often people find help in church—faith, hope and purpose for living. All of this takes place in an atmosphere of reverence, where a man contemplating suicide may be averted from it, a woman desiring to break up a home can be changed from her selfish ambitions, and a young fellow asking for help can be given strength to overcome a habit. "Be still, and know that I am God . . . In returning and rest shall ye be saved; in quietness and in confidence shall be your strength" (Ps. 46:10; Isa. 30:15).

In church we take time to confess our sins and receive pardon. And when you join with other Christians in prayer, you realize that they too are in the same boat. They too are struggling to win battles, they too need to confess their sins, they too need to pray for forgiveness, they too need the Lord's help for their lives. We know that where two or three are gathered in His name, Jesus is present too! So if the worship service gives people bread instead of stones, they will be spiritually fed and nourished.

Now if you should make your way back to church, and I sincerely hope that you will, one thing will be necessary. Set your own patterns. Refuse to be put into any mold that is prescribed for you. You do not have to run with every group or do what everybody does in the institution. All Christians do not have to act the same. You are an individual. You will serve God as He has called you. I don't mean that you must stick out like a sore thumb, but I mean that you don't have to be set into the same mold someone else is. You are first of all responsible to the Lord who loves you as an individual. He wants you to be yourself, or else He would not have made you an unique person.

I know of a couple who went through a similar period of questioning for almost ten years. It looked as if they would never return to the church, nor had they any such intentions. They attended rarely, and then mostly due to their children who were in the youth program. Now they are back. I wish I knew why. I don't know why. But I suspect there may be a couple of answers.

For one thing, they've discovered that they missed something that had previously been a regular part of their lives. They missed worship and got a little tired of the liberties they were taking. They went away almost every weekend, but it just did not gel any more. It was fun for a while, but if you do the same thing too often, it isn't fun any more. During this period it wasn't possible for me to even suggest that they return to church. Threats were useless of course, and even a loving, persistent urging was rejected.

A great contributing factor in their return was their ability to discuss their questions. After sometime completely separated from church, they became part of a group in which they were free to raise their objections in an atmosphere of acceptance. And they found others with similar concerns, some within and some outside of the establishment. I suspect this had quite an influence on their change of heart.

By the way—this couple is not at retirement age, nor are their children full grown yet. To the contrary. They've discovered that life begins at forty and their children are struggling through the teen years.

One other point. This couple has grown from a narrow, confining, threatening hell-fire and brimstone Christianity to a deeper, broader understanding of the faith. They are still conservatives, but they see more of the love and grace of God. They have grown in their understanding of God.

Aren't you both groping beyond the fundamental, confining patterns which were established in your youth? Haven't you tried for some time to retain these patterns, somewhat unsuccessfully? And since you were not successful, you have begun to lash out at the institution which gave you these restrictive dogmas. Could it be, therefore, that many of your objections are due to your dissatisfactions with your selves?

Consider this word from Scripture: "Just as you received Christ, so go on living in Him—in simple faith. Grow out of Him as a plant grows out of the soil it is planted in, becoming more and more sure of your 'ground', and your lives will overflow with joy and thankfulness" (Col. 2:6,7, Phillips). You have received Christ by faith. Now, says the Apostle Paul, go on not necessarily in fundamental traditions, but *in Christ*. Proceed in a vibrant and meaningful faith. As you have been rooted in Him, so grow. Experience His daily mercy and suffering love "and your lives will overflow with joy and thankfulness."

I don't know whether you can accept any of these thoughts that I have shared with you in this letter, Walt and Lucy. But since you have voiced your concerns to me, I have attempted to have you understand yourselves better, and also (perhaps) indicated some steps you can take.

I am confident that He who is Lord of us all will show you the way.

Sincerely, in His name,

16

*Letter to
Two Conscientious
Christians*

Dear Dave and Judy,

A minister doesn't get a letter like yours very often! Not too
many people are asking questions like yours, not even Christians whom you would consider pillars of the church. You
want to know how you can become more committed to Christ,
more dedicated; how you can live the Christian life with more
concern, more love—in short be better Christians.

At first glance yours seems a noble and worthy request, and
I know you raise it seriously and sincerely. Still I cannot help
but make a comparison with the one and only serious request
that came to Jesus during His earthly ministry. You will
excuse me if I make this comparison, because I'm leading up to
something.

Once a rich young man came to Jesus with the question:
"Good Master, what good thing shall I do, that I may have
eternal life" (Matt. 19:16)? Jesus told him to keep the commandments. He answered our Lord that since his childhood he
had kept them and lived according to the law of God. This was

kindergarten stuff to him. What more important steps should he take?

Jesus answered him that these commandments implied more than this rich young man had seen in them, and that if he wanted to become a Christian he would have to sell all his possessions, distribute them to the poor (his neighbors) and follow Him. In short, Jesus asked for total dedication and commitment. As you well remember, this was far too much for that fellow as he walked away sadly.

Now, what would *you* do if Jesus answered you in this manner? Would you sell everything and give it all to the poor? I'm not saying that Jesus demands this of you or that I am demanding it, but what would your reaction be *if* He did? That's the point I was leading up to. And if you should rebel at that thought, if you are unwilling to respond to Jesus Christ, you put yourself in the same position as this rich young fellow in our story, as well as other disciples who left when the teaching of Jesus became too tough! (See John 6:66).

Jesus makes great demands. Hearing them often blunts their edge, but they are still as sharp as a razor. If we are to be His disciples, we must choose Him, seek first His kingdom, forsake all others, deny ourselves, take up our cross and follow Him! We must count the cost of discipleship which involves utter dedication, utter commitment, utter devotion. No small price to pay! But whether we like it or not, this is what Jesus says.

So, you come with your question: "What should we do to become better, more involved, more loving Christians?" The first answer must be total commitment to Christ: "Whoever does not carry his own cross and come after me cannot be my disciple . . . None of you can be my disciple unless he gives up everything he has" (Luke 14:27,33, ABS).

How do you commit yourself? That's the question! How do you grow? How can you become the person you want to become?

122

There are many standard answers for this, of course. I may as well list some of them for you. "Go to church", say some. And that's true. As you worship and pray, as you hear the Word of God read and proclaimed, as you sing and fellowship with others, faith, hope and new insight will be given you. We should not forsake the assembling of ourselves together, for where two or three are gathered in His name, there Christ is in the midst.

Others will tell you to read the Bible. Your answers are found in the revealed Word of God. True again. "Search the scriptures; . . . they are they which testify of me" (John 5:39). And I will not be able to spell out for you how to commit yourself, but as you read the Bible you will receive light. There is a beautiful passage in Job which reads in part: "Acquaint now yourself with him and be at peace . . . Receive the law from his mouth and lay up his words in thine heart . . . and the light shall shine upon thy ways" (Job 22:21-28).

Other voices urge you to pray, even to pray without ceasing. And they are right also. For we grow in our understanding of God through communicating with Him.

Then there are those who emphasize the work of the Holy Spirit. They tell you to pray for the filling of the Spirit and to receive Him in all His fullness. Many of these Christians are living a joyful, positive Christian life, and they have found it by pursuing the gift of the Spirit. Some have received special gifts such as tongues—praising God in ecstatic utterances. And the New Testament says: "Be filled with the Spirit" (Eph. 5:18), which should be literally translated "be being filled with the Spirit." It is a command to be receptive daily and continually to the progressive control of the Spirit of God.

There are yet other Christians who concentrate on small groups, Christian cells. This was the secret of the early Christians' fervor and dedication, as they witnessed that phenomenal growth in the first century. The book of Acts tells the story of these small fellowships. In such groups there can be an openness, a freedom and growth which will lead to further commitment.

Finally, some make the point that you should forget about yourself and serve your fellow man. Love your neighbor, help the poor, work in God's vineyard. That's how you will develop in your faith. Don't be so concerned about your own spiritual progress, but think about others. And, of course, there is truth here.

Christ meets us not only in worship where two or three are gathered in His name, not only in the Word of God when we search the Scriptures and discover that they speak of Him, He also meets us in our ministries to people, for "inasmuch as ye have done it unto one of the least of these my brethren, ye have done it unto me" (Matt. 25:40). He meets us in worship, in the Word and in our Christian works.

But actually, Judy and Dave, if you are conscientious about growing spiritually, none of these answers is sufficient in itself. They only have value when you put them all together into a delicious Christian stew. All these ingredients are a part of dedication—worship, reading the Bible, prayer, living in the power of the Spirit, honest small group fellowships and work in God's world.

The Word without the Spirit remains sterile, for the letter alone kills. The Spirit without the Word gives emotional feelings.

Prayer without worship becomes selfish piety. The church without social service is pious indulgence.

Small groups without the Spirit turn into frothy discussions. Social action without the Bible becomes altruistic do-goodism.

You see? *All* these ingredients contribute to Christian maturity. There is no single, quick formula. To this you may reply that I have given you all the old answers. You know this already. Is there anything else? Anything new that can be said? Perhaps.

The very fact that you're in earnest is in your favor. Didn't Jesus say that those who hunger and thirst for righteousness will be satisfied? The poor in spirit receive the kingdom. Not those who are rich in spirit, who know it all, who have all the answers, but those who confess their poverty, who do not have the power, who come to the Lord every day for grace and love and His Spirit. That's part of the answer, isn't it? "Give us *this day* our daily bread." And not only bread, for "man shall not live by bread alone, but by every word that proceedeth out of the mouth of God" (Matt. 4:4).

Another point, although it's obvious, is this. You need to remember that you will never reach the goal. We want so much to *achieve*. We want to accomplish, so that we can boast of our accomplishments! That's the way man runs the show, but it's not Christianity. There is no boasting before God. As there is no instant formula for Christian success (like instant coffee), so there is no completed perfection in this life, even for saints!

"I do not consider myself to have 'arrived', spiritually, nor do I consider myself already perfect. But I keep going on, grasping ever more firmly that purpose for which Christ grasped me" (Phil. 3:12, Phillips). Paul was always reaching forward. He was dissatisfied with his achievements. Let this encourage you. Whenever a Christian believes he has reached a spiritual plateau, he is on dangerous ground. That very moment the earth begins to crumble under his feet, and he will soon experience a fall that may prove disastrous.

But what does the New Testament tell us about growth? A number of things, yet I want to call to your attention one arresting phrase: "Grow in grace, and in the knowledge of our Lord and Savior Jesus Christ" (II Pet. 3:18). To grow in the knowledge of Jesus Christ is easy to interpret. You learn of

Christ by reading His revealed Word. But what does it mean to grow in grace?

We know that grace (unmerited favor from God to unworthy men) is given to the humble not the proud, to the sinful not the righteous, to those who are in need. Only those who confess their sins, open themselves to the grace of God, only those who express their emptiness, can be filled. Only those who hunger and thirst for righteousness will be satisfied. Do you see the point? If you are to grow in grace as a Christian, this means that you must *continually* express your need for God.

Martin Luther once said that we are all beggars of the grace of God. What is a beggar? He comes with open hands. As Christian beggars we come with open hands to God, expecting Him to give us grace. If we approach Him with full hands, with our own spiritual accomplishments, there is nothing He can give us. If we hold our hands behind our backs with all our little sins in them, while making pious prayers, how can He honor those prayers? Beggars may not be choosers, but they are receivers.

Does that help? Does that give you some insight into these old words—commitment, devotion, dedication, decision? We know what we should do, but we need handles to take hold of. I suppose I have omitted certain aspects of the deeper life, as some call it. Frankly, I don't like that term. What we should seek is a life with God, to learn of Jesus, to be led by the Spirit. The deeper life places the emphasis on the self. I'd like to place it on God. We are not to pray "hallowed be *my* name," but "hallowed by *thy* name."

There is one more word that I would like to emphasize, which has been very helpful in my own thinking. That is the word "relationship."

You are a child of God. God is your heavenly Father. Doesn't this mean that as His child, you seek to please Him, to do His will, to discover what He wants of you? Wherever you begin to think of a relationship with God, this opens up new avenues of thought. Some people, you know, are always talking about God as the Lord, and they (quite unconsciously probably) consider themselves his servants. When God is your Lord, you are but His servant. But when you accept Jesus' teaching that you are no longer His servant but His child, and that God is your Father, you enter a different way of living. And remember, Jesus continually called God, "Father." We are accepted as His children too, by faith. And all this means *relationship.*

God's Son Jesus has revealed all that God wants you to know. Listen to Him. Put it into practice. Take the Scriptures seriously. He teaches a new way of life. I know that some of His teaching seems to place impossible demands upon you. Nevertheless, that is the narrow way we are to travel as God's children, and none of our cheap, easy-come-easy-go interpretations of Christianity will be adequate. Relationship is the word!

All this can only become a reality through the Holy Spirit—God present with us. He makes that relationship real. He is given to us to empower us for living. He is the one who will lead us into all truth. He creates within us the fruit of the Spirit: "Love, joy, peace, longsuffering, gentleness, goodness, faith, meekness, temperance" (Gal. 5:22,23). He is what the sap is to the branch, if it is to live in the vine.

So, dear Dave and Judy, I hope I've given you a few suggestions in this letter, but there are no short cuts to Christian maturity. I'm so glad you belong to the family of God, and I'm certain that your hearts' desires will be fulfilled as you walk and live in the Spirit as beggars of the grace of God!

"May the God of peace make you holy through and through. May you be kept in soul and mind and body in spotless

127

integrity until the coming of our Lord Jesus Christ. He Who calls you is utterly faithful and He will finish what He has set out to do" (I Thess. 5:23,24, Phillips).

In His name,